Elements of International Trade and Payments

Geoffrey Whitehead BSc (Econ)

Woodhead-Faulkner
New York London Toronto Sydney Tokyo Singapore

Published by Woodhead-Faulkner Limited
Simon & Schuster International Group
Fitzwilliam House, 32 Trumpington Street
Cambridge CB2 1QY, England

First published 1983
Second impression 1988
Third impression 1990

Designed by Geoff Green

Typesetting by
Wyvern Typesetting Limited, Bristol

Printed in Great Britain by
St Edmundsbury Press Limited
Bury St Edmunds, Suffolk

Introduction to series

In the last 40 years international trade has grown enormously under the influence of international agreements which began in 1944 at the Bretton Woods Conference. These agreements recognised that all nations, whatever their economic organisation, must trade if they are to achieve prosperity. Some degree of international specialisation is inevitable, if only because some countries have raw materials that others do not have, some have climates favourable to particular crops, and some have skills and expertise that others have not yet acquired. The result is that we are now faced with a situation in which every firm must consider an overseas market as a major part of its natural market, while production for the home market must meet serious competition from foreign suppliers. It follows that an understanding of the foundations of overseas trade is of enormous importance to the commercial success of every firm, and there is a great need for trained personnel with this type of background.

In order to ensure an adequate supply of trained, professional personnel in this important field of international trade, there have developed over the years specialised vocational courses by the appropriate bodies who represent the various professions engaged in international trading. The professional bodies concerned include the Institute of Export, the Institute of Freight Forwarders, the Society of Shipping Executives and the Institute of Marketing. These four bodies have agreed and recognised a set of syllabuses for the Foundation Course in Overseas Trade, which also forms the basis for Part I of their own qualifying examinations. This has been achieved by offering an optional specialist paper in marketing. Students who successfully complete the Foundation Course in Overseas Trade will be permitted to embark upon more advanced courses of study leading to full membership of their respective Institutes.

The 'Elements of Overseas Trade Series' seeks to cover the four syllabuses in this new Foundation Course in Overseas Trade and the Institutes' joint Part I examinations. There are five titles in the series, since cargo insurance (part of the transportation and documentation syllabus) has been considered in a separate volume. The five titles are:

- *Elements of Cargo Insurance*, Dennis Badger and Geoffrey Whitehead;
- *Elements of Export Law*, Geoffrey Whitehead;
- *Elements of International Trade and Payments*, Geoffrey Whitehead;
- *Elements of Transportation and Documentation*, Geoffrey Whitehead and Ralph Bugg;
- *Elements of Export Marketing*, John Stapleton.

The last chapter of each book contains a section entitled 'Organising your studies'. Students may find it helpful to read this section before commencing their courses. Also included are details of the names, addresses and telephone numbers of professional organisations in the export field.

Preface

The purpose of this book is to describe the framework within which international trade is conducted, the terms and conditions imposed by the parties engaged in it, the ways trade is financed and the detailed arrangements for payments. In order to assist those entering the field of export trade for the first time, information has been presented in tabular or checklist form wherever possible to display alternative methods of trading, terms of trade and so on. Situations have been viewed from the standpoint of each of the parties, where this is helpful, to bring out the legal implications of various activities.

As an introductory text it is designed to help the reader insert a foot into the export door, by providing a coherent background to the activities of exporters, and to give basic training in pre-shipment finance, methods of payment, currency transactions and export credit insurance.

International trade is a restless activity, with developments occurring all the time. It is essential to keep abreast of changes in export finance by regular perusal of the business and specialist press. Membership of a professional organisation is particularly desirable, and the addresses and telephone numbers of relevant Institutes are given in the final chapter of the book.

Geoffrey Whitehead

Acknowledgements

In preparing this book I have been greatly assisted by a number of firms and organisations, and I am most grateful for their help.

Permission was kindly given by the SITPRO Board to reproduce their Master Document and two documentary collection forms and by Formecon Services Ltd to reproduce a bill of exchange and other documents. Barclays Export Services Ltd gave me much helpful advice and permission to refer to their booklets *Export Finance* and *Finance for Imports*, and the Export Credits Guarantee Department agreed to reference being made to their *ECGD Services* booklet.

The Institute of Export, the Institute of Freight Forwarders, the Society of Shipping Executives, the Institute of Marketing and the Chartered Insurance Institute kindly supplied examination syllabuses, to which reference has been made in preparing the text.

The International Chamber of Commerce gave permission to reproduce in full the texts of *Uniform Customs and Practice for Documentary Credits* (ICC publication no. 290) and *Uniform Rules for Collections* (ICC publication no. 322). Copyright © of these publications is held by the International Chamber of Commerce, 38 Cours Albert 1er, 75008 Paris. These and other publications are available from the International Chamber of Commerce and from the British National Committee of the ICC, Centre Point, 103 New Oxford Street, London WC1A 1QB (tel: 01-240 5558) and National Committees of the ICC throughout the world.

Finally, I would like to thank Ralph Bugg of Thurrock Technical College for reading and commenting on certain sections of the manuscript. His forthright comments on the practical difficulties encountered in export trade were most helpful.

Contents

Chapter 1
A survey of international trade

1.1 International trade in the framework of the world economy

We live in a world where there are three main types of economy existing side by side. We call these economies (*a*) free enterprise economies, (*b*) mixed economies, and (*c*) controlled economies.

Free enterprise economies are ones where there is a minimum of government control; trade and industry are largely run by private firms. The best example perhaps is the United States of America, but many of the developing countries have this type of economy.

Mixed economies are ones where there are some state-run industries, but a great many industries and most trading activities are in the hands of private firms. The best example of this type of country is the United Kingdom, but to some extent all advanced nations and many developing nations have at least some state-run industries.

Controlled economies are ones where the whole economy is state-run, including all the trading activity except for tiny pockets of free enterprise – for example the ordinary peasant may be allowed to sell a few spare vegetables for cash. This sort of economy is generally communist-controlled, and international trade is largely carried on by state trading enterprises which are very powerful and extremely tough bargainers. Of course, when they do buy they are placing huge orders worth millions of pounds. The typical example of this type of economy is that of the Soviet Union.

To some extent all economies are mixed economies. Even the most ardent free-enterprise countries have areas where central government either exercises direct control or manipulates the economy by monetary or fiscal (taxation) means. Conversely, the most centralised state system breaks down at the point where the measures to control private economic activity become ludicrously expensive for the effect achieved, and it is no accident that some of the most prosperous communist bloc countries are those that have relaxed state control in economic affairs.

Over the last 25 years or so there has developed one particular type of organisation which is very influential at an international level. It is the multinational company. Such companies operate, by consent, within many nations and bring prosperity to many economies, but their ability to switch resources and production from one country to another has brought them a good deal of criticism. They have to some extent made the picture of international trade less clear, since they operate within many nations.

International trade operates within the framework laid down by these different types of economy. If we are trading with a free enterprise nation, we may expect to meet many nationals of that country, moving freely around the world, prepared to visit us to do business or to welcome us abroad. If we are trading with a controlled economy, we shall expect to do business only with accredited representatives of their state trading organisation. We shall expect them to be very knowledgeable and experienced for they have their whole country's trade passing through their hands, but we shall also expect them to be rather formal in their approach and to some extent tied up in 'red' tape.

1.2 The United Kingdom as a trading nation

In 1760 when the Industrial Revolution began the United Kingdom had less than 7 million people, vast reserves of coal – the chief source of power – and a plentiful supply of iron, tin, lead and copper. She was an exporter of corn and other grains, agriculturally self-sufficient, produced a large wool crop and was beginning to receive a plentiful supply of foreign produce from subject peoples all over the world.

In 1982 her population exceeded 55 million. Although North Sea oil and gas have made her largely self-sufficient in these vital fuels, at least for a few years, many formerly prosperous coal mines have been closed as uneconomic. She is no longer self-sufficient in any of the primary products like metals, timber, agricultural produce or the products of animal husbandry, while her manufacturers and even her service industries like banking and insurance are meeting fierce competition from abroad. Since 1960 the remaining colonial countries have been granted independence and the sterling area has been reduced to the point where it includes only the Channel Isles, the Isle of Man, Eire and Gibraltar. Even the Isle of Man is considering leaving the sterling area, to facilitate its role as a tax haven.

The contrast between these two situations is striking. We have far more people to support, with far fewer natural resources. We can support them only if we trade internationally, buying the raw materials that we need and manufacturing them into more sophisticated products for sale abroad. We can also offer our other skills in the transport, distribution, banking and risk-carrying fields. To the extent that other nations will allow us to perform these tasks for them, we can earn foreign exchange to buy the products that we need, including food and other items for home consumption and use.

This is not the place to go into the theory of international trade, although an understanding of this theory is of great use to practical exporters and importers in helping them to understand what is happening. Those readers who wish to follow this theory will find a clear explanation of it in *Economics Made Simple*, details of which are given in Chapter 9. It is sufficient here to understand the basic facts revealed in the contrasting situations in 1760 and 1982 described above. We must export or we shall die but equally we must import or we shall die, for without the imports we cannot export. It is therefore better to say that we must engage in international trade or die. Later in this chapter (see page 4) we shall contrast the import and export positions, and discuss the balance of payments that arises as a result.

1.3 The pattern of United Kingdom international trade

Trade may be divided into 'visible trade' and 'invisible trade'. Visible trade is trade in goods, which can actually be seen passing through our ports and airports, entering or leaving the country. Invisible trade is trade in services. We usually think here of such items as transport, banking, tourism and insurance, but another 'invisible' which is more closely related to visible trade is the 'licensing' of foreigners to build our manufactured goods in their own countries. If we licensed China to produce Harrier jump jets, for example, making available to her all the technological knowledge required for the manufacture of the aircraft, then the sums she paid for the use of this know-how would be an invisible item of trade. Instead of importing aluminium, etc., and manufacturing aircraft for export we would simply receive a cash payment.

The figures given in Table 1.1 and 1.2 are taken from the *United Kingdom Balance of Payments 1981*, an official publication called *The Pink Book*, because it has a pink cover. (No more recent data on visible trade were available at the time of writing because of industrial action in 1982.)

Table 1.1 UK trade 1980

	£ million
Visible exports (fob)	47,389
Visible imports (fob)	46,211
Favourable balance of visible trade	1,178
Favourable balance of invisibles	2,028
Final (favourable) balance	3,206

Reproduced by courtesy of the Controller General, Her Majesty's Stationery Office.

Table 1.1 shows the satisfactory position of United Kingdom trade in the year 1980 despite the difficult world economic climate and the rising rate of unemployment in the United Kingdom. However, this satisfactory position was very largely dependent on the discovery of North Sea oil and gas, which changed a serious deficit on visible trade into a surplus once the oil and gas were fully on stream.

Table 1.2 UK visible trade 1980

Imports	£ million	Exports	£ million
Food, drink & tobacco	5,619	Food, drink & tobacco	3,241
Raw materials	3,413	Raw materials	1,467
Fuels and lubricants	6,589	Fuels and lubricants	6,418
Manufactured goods	16,862	Manufactured goods	20,727
Semi-manufactured goods	12,523	Semi-manufactured goods	14,152
Other items	1,205	Other items	1,384
	46,211		47,389

Final (favourable) balance therefore £1,178 million

Reproduced by courtesy of the Controller General, Her Majesty's Stationery Office.

The detailed figures for visible trade given in Table 1.2 show that the United Kingdom is still a major importer of food, drink and tobacco (net imports of £2,378 million), basic raw materials (net imports of £1,946 million) and, despite a huge output of North Sea oil and gas, a net importer of fuels and lubricants (£171 million). Some idea of the impact of North Sea oil on the balance of payments position can be gathered from the contrast with the year 1974, when the total balance on visible trade was an adverse balance of £5,234 million, of which net oil imports accounted for £3,429 million. Another interesting aspect of these figures is the extent of the imports of manufactured and semi-manufactured goods (£29,385 million).

We would expect, from the situation of the United Kingdom in 1982 described earlier, that this country would have to import a great deal of food to feed her population of 55 million people, and a great deal of raw materials to make up for the shortage of these products, largely exhausted since the Industrial Revolution. What we might have expected is that we could at least make our own manufactured goods. Instead, we are clearly importing an enormous quantity of foreign goods which we could easily make ourselves. The explanation is that in the present climate of world opinion free trade is viewed as a very desirable thing. Under the General Agreement on Tariffs and Trade (GATT) most advanced nations have consented to the free circulation of many products within minimal tariff barriers, while in the European Community (as in any other trading bloc) the basic idea is that free trade exists between members of the Community. We cannot therefore shut out German or French or Danish goods, except, of course, by being so efficient that foreign goods are more highly priced and more unreliable than our home products. This is just not true at present. Clearly this is bringing us into a field of economic debate which is not really appropriate for this book, however vital it may be for the nation.

The one conclusion we can draw from this brief glance at the pattern of United Kingdom trade is that above all we need as a nation to earn every penny of foreign exchange that we possibly can and that is why this Foundation Course in Overseas Trade is of such importance. It will enable you to improve the part you can play in raising the general efficiency of our trading, enabling us to win extra trade or at least preserve our present share of the world's markets, and to that extent your study will have been worth while. We must engage in overseas trade if our standard of living is to be maintained. Many people feel that they have too low a standard of living, and the aspirations of such lower-paid citizens can be realised only if we actually increase the range of our international trade, and trade with greater efficiency.

1.4 The changing pattern of United Kingdom trade and markets

In the last 25 years United Kingdom trade has changed enormously, both in the things that we sell abroad and in the markets to which they are sold. These changes may be reviewed by looking at some of the important political events which have brought about these changes. Without going too deeply into the matter the following points are of importance.

1.4.1 *The ending of the colonial system*

Here the chief feature perhaps is the tendency of newly independent nations to shop around for the cheapest buy – a process which often leads them to switch from buying British goods to buying Japanese, Chinese, Russian or other goods. The granting of privileged credit terms or even interest-free loans by these nations has increased this tendency. Where we have made loans – and regrettably this has been on a decreasing scale in recent years – we have tended to permit the loans to be used to buy goods anywhere, i.e. the loans have not been tied to the sale of British goods. This policy has been in line with the enlightened views of bodies such as the United Nations, but it has adversely affected our foreign trade.

1.4.2 *The growth of the European Economic Community and UK admission to it*

The European Community has grown faster than any other market in the last 15 years. The strength of a market reflects two things (*i*) its size in population terms, and (*ii*) the affluence of that population. The European Community consists of about 350 million people, all of whom are relatively affluent, so it has become a very large market indeed. The rules of the Community require trade to pass between members wherever possible, rather than to outsiders. This has meant that United Kingdom trade is being diverted more and more from traditional suppliers to European suppliers. Good examples are sugar, butter, cheese and beef, tending to come more and more from Europe than from the Caribbean, Australia and New Zealand. We are similarly selling a large proportion of our manufactures to EEC countries, although our efficiency in some industries is too low for us to compete effectively.

1.4.3 *The development of Third World countries into manufacturing nations*

It is inevitable that developing nations will seek to industrialise themselves. The industrialisation of these countries has robbed the United Kingdom of many of its overseas markets. The outstanding example of this is Japanese development into a first class world power, but the development of Hong Kong, Singapore and India has affected the United Kingdom more in certain industries, particularly in the cotton and the garment trades but also in electronics and the carrying trades.

The fragmentation of Africa, while not striking a blow at any particular industry, has made United Kingdom exports to that continent subject to many pressures, from downright expropriation to severe competition, quite apart from our own desire to assist their processes of development by agreeing to permit them to market their manufactured products in the United Kingdom.

1.4.4 *The energy shortage*

The 'energy shortage' may be only temporary, but it has caused a major change in market patterns. The oil-producing nations have secured an increased share of the world's total wealth, at the expense of the non-oil-producing nations. Although the United Kingdom has now become largely self-sufficient in oil, she has been affected very severely by world energy shortages and has been very involved in 'recycling' oil funds. We have increased our sales to the oil-producing countries of sophisticated products and services, in an attempt to earn back some of the extra revenue they are receiving.

1.5 Sources of information on markets

1.5.1 *Official United Kingdom sources*

The Department of Trade has a huge organisation for helping firms seriously interested in exporting. The information is provided under the direction of the British Overseas Trade Board (BOTB). The services are fully described in a publication, *Export Handbook*, which is available from HMSO, price £4.95, or from booksellers.

The BOTB operates in the following way:

(*a*) There is a network of *11 regional offices* (whose addresses are given in the *Export Handbook*) which provide assistance locally for firms seeking advice and access to the BOTB's services.

(*b*) There are *8 market branches* of the Overseas Trade Divisions, all located at the Department of Trade Headquarters,

1 Victoria Street, London SW1H 0ET. The branches and their telephone numbers are:

North America branch	01-215 5647
Exports to Europe branch	01-215 5336
East Europe branch	01-215 5258
Middle East branch	01-215 5501
North Africa, Caribbean and Latin American branch	01-215 3273
Sub-Saharan Africa branch	01-215 3338
China and SE Asia branch	01-215 5278
NE and SE Asia and Australasia branch:	
NE Asia	01-215 5625
SE Asia	01-215 3261
Australasia	01-215 5318

These branches will provide advice on individual markets, including information on tariffs and important regulations.

(*c*) *SMIL and PDS*. SMIL is the Statistical and Market Intelligence Library; PDS is the Product Data Store.

These two organisations provide facilities for desk research on markets worldwide, with microfiche readers and document copying facilities. The services available are fully described in the *Export Handbook*.

(*d*) *A market advisory service*. This service, for which a charge is made, provides a report prepared by the Commercial Section of the Diplomatic Service Post Overseas on the potential of the product or services offered in that particular market, including advice on effective local representation.

(*e*) *THE* (Technical Help to Exporters) is a BOTB-sponsored department of the British Standards Institute which helps exporters comply with technical standards in overseas markets.

(*f*) *Mission schemes*. The Outward and Inward Missions Schemes offer support and financial assistance to businessmen travelling abroad or bringing in foreign businessmen likely to influence exports.

(*g*) *Joint-venture schemes*. These offer small display areas and shell-stands at display pavilions, British Weeks, etc., to those seeking to develop an export market.

(*h*) *EIS*. The Export Intelligence Service distributes information daily on a highly selective basis about tenders called for and other opportunities in overseas markets. Subscribers register the categories of products and services they can offer in 18 categories with 7,000 commodity headings. The computer then automatically matches their business needs with opportunities notified by 200 overseas posts.

(*i*) *MEGS*. The Market Entry Guarantee Scheme helps small and medium-sized businesses break into new overseas markets by funding advertising and promotion campaigns to a considerable extent – recouping its costs out of a share in the benefits if the promotion is successful.

A full account of BOTB services is given in *Export Handbook*, which is really required reading for all exporters.

1.5.2 *Other official sources*

The Embassies, Legations and Consulates of foreign countries, and the High Commissions of Commonwealth countries have parallel organisations to our own official bodies, which issue information about export opportunities in their own countries, and products and contracts for which tenders are invited. Most of them have Trading Corporations, or Purchasing Associations, resident Commercial Counsellors and other official advisers who will respond to enquiries to make approaches on products in which they are interested.

1.5.3 *Trade sources*

There is a very wide range of non-government overseas trade organisations in the United Kingdom which are able to assist United Kingdom exporters. The most important, perhaps, are the overseas Chambers of Commerce, the addresses of which can be found in the *Export Handbook* referred to earlier, and available from the British Overseas Trade Board. Most trade associations have departments with a responsibility for promoting exports, and members of a particular industry cannot do better than approach their own trade association for information which is likely to be highly relevant to their own particular situations. Such associations know all the snags that other members have met in particular countries.

Direct approaches can also be made to buying houses in the United Kingdom representing overseas stores. The names and addresses of the principal buying houses are listed in the *Export Handbook*, indicating the countries whose stores they represent. These buying houses often act as consolidators for the stores, buying lines from numerous United Kingdom manufacturers and making up full container loads for shipment.

Besides foreign trade organisations in this country, there are the British trade organisations set up overseas. The British Chamber of Commerce has mutual links with almost all parts of the world, producing weekly letters or monthly journals. Membership is inexpensive and ensures that a stream of relevant information about a particular country's changing situation is received. Once again the *Export Handbook* has a useful compendium of addresses.

1.6 The overseas trade executive

Those who aspire to become executives in overseas trade, running export or import departments, must establish a sound basis of knowledge which will justify their appointments. The aim is not just to describe the nuts and bolts of exporting, but also to show how these nuts and bolts fit into the whole machinery of international trade. Of course one wants to know in the most accurate detail how one's own particular firm deals with each aspect of the work, but this must be supplemented by an appreciation of the total picture – first of all with regard to the trade of the United Kingdom with the particular country concerned, and secondly to the overall world scene and the balance of payments it involves.

It follows that a joint study is necessary of the practice of exporting and importing and the theory of international trade. This last phrase does not mean the economic theory referred to earlier, even though that is interesting and helpful. Rather it means that general background picture of world trade, the trends that are developing, the influences at work to improve or worsen our firm's position. Management does not operate in a stable, unchanging situation; the situation is dynamic and competitive. In the home market we can perhaps protect ourselves with restrictive practices of various sorts. In international trade there is no such protection – we operate in an atmosphere open to all the winds that blow. We may, with a certain amount of ingenuity, arrange 'hedging' contracts of one sort or another to protect us from the prevailing icy blasts, but hedges are expensive to plant.

One way to be prepared is to be fully informed about the countries we are dealing with. A regular review of the relevant publications; membership of the appropriate bodies which collect, collate and distribute statistics and report on changing laws and regulations; circulation of cuttings to all members of staff who ought to be made aware of developments and regular attendance at seminars and staff conferences on particular aspects of the international scene are helpful. Many banks publish regular circulars on changes in the countries where they operate. Such information forms useful background knowledge, and may spark off enquiries which lead to an extension of the market, or to cancelling it altogether if it appears likely that foreign exchange will not be made available to ensure settlement in the future.

Export executives must therefore do their best to take advantage of dynamic situations. They must lead, not follow. In boom times they must have an eye open for the first signs of a downturn in the economies of the countries where they trade. In slumps it is often possible to capitalise on the slump situation and be better prepared as a result for the next upsurge of activity.

1.7 How overseas trade is conducted

The pattern of arrangements for conducting overseas trade is intricate. There are many solutions to the problems, and which solution is most appropriate depends upon the situation of each firm. Firms range from very small-scale firms embarking upon their first venture in overseas trade to multinational companies who will be well placed to judge the situation and select their best channel for exports or imports. The chief channels for overseas trade may be listed as follows.

(*a*) *Selling to export houses*. Export houses may be merchants buying goods to sell abroad, or confirming houses buying goods for foreign importers, or export agents prepared to act for the exporter in countries where they have expertise.

(*b*) *Selling by agents in the foreign country*. Here the agent's existing selling base is used to market the firm's products overseas. Similarly, UK businessmen may deal with this type of agent when buying foreign goods in this country.

(*c*) *Selling from the United Kingdom direct to the overseas customer*. This system is possible only for the larger company prepared to exploit the foreign market directly by an export-orientated selling organisation with specialist staff.

(*d*) *Selling through a branch office or a subsidiary company*. Here the exporter sets up his own organisation, training and supervising nationals of the foreign country to act on his behalf.

(*e*) *Joint selling schemes*. Some firms join in a scheme to market products overseas and share expenses. The British Overseas Trade Board also runs joint-venture projects of this type.

A detailed account of the advantages and disadvantages of each of these channels is given in Table 1.3.

Table 1.3 Channels of overseas trade – advantages and disadvantages

This chart deals with the export side of overseas trade. Those interested in the import side will find the same institutions operating but must consider their activities from the opposite point of view.

Exporter		Channel of overseas trade (The description in brackets explains its organisation)	Overseas importer	
Advantages	Disadvantages		Advantages	Disadvantages
1. Merchant may initiate advances and thus open up new markets. 2. No need for own export organisation. 3. No problems with payment – becomes virtually a home transaction.	1. Goodwill lost to merchant house as own identity may not be revealed. 2. Producing in the dark to some extent as to true needs and potential of market. 3. Unable to influence market and create further sales.	**Export merchant** (The merchant buys goods as a principal, selling them on his own account. He may do this against the known requirements of overseas customers, or because he has made an arrangement with you to promote your goods abroad, or because he is an expert in 'compensation deals', i.e. 'barter' or 'switch' deals. He carries the risk of carrying goods through time. He fixes prices to the importer.)	1. Has confidence in the export merchant. 2. Can obtain redress of grievances from known merchant. 3. May be able to get credit facilities. 4. May get choice of products from a merchant dealing in many lines.	1. Price may be a little higher than by other methods.
1. Credit carried by confirming house, who also pays promptly and in home currency. 2. Confirming house usually packs and arranges to transport goods. 3. Often a closer link with the overseas customer since the confirming house is only an agent.	Same as 2 and 3 above.	**Confirming house** (The export house confirms the orders placed by overseas buyers, thus acting effectively as a principal and assuming the responsibility of paying for the goods on shipment, and carrying the credit risk.)	1. Is able to place an order to his exact specifications. 2. The confirming house ensures that the goods are as required, and *may* be liable for redress of grievances if negligent. 3. Importer may get credit.	

Table 1.3 (cont.)

Exporter		Channel of overseas trade (The description in brackets explains its organisation)	Overseas importer	
Advantages	Disadvantages		Advantages	Disadvantages
1. Agent knows market, language, etc., thus reducing need for specialist export organisation.	1. Agent may act for several exporters and not pursue business aggressively. 2. Exporter must arrange dispatch and transport, etc.	**Overseas agent** (The agent uses his existing selling base to market his principal's products. He may sell on consignment terms, rendering an Account Sales. He often acts as a *del credere* agent, carrying the bad debts risk.)	1. Presence of agent means importer has direct contact. 2. Agent may give after-sales service and liaises with exporter on importer's behalf.	
1. Full export department facilities give direct projection of company image and full feedback of market impact and potential. 2. Makes possible accurate production planning. 3. Develops export expertise. 4. Full profit accrues to exporter, not intermediaries.	1. Full export organisation required.	**Direct selling to overseas customer** (Exporter uses his home organisation to contact foreign customers directly.)	1. Strong personal links with exporter, so direct access for complaints. 2. Direct negotiation on prices.	1. Negotiations conducted at long range. 2. Possible language difficulties.

(*This table is continued overleaf.*)

Table 1.3 (cont.)

Exporter		Channel of overseas trade (The description in brackets explains its organisation)	Overseas importer	
Advantages	Disadvantages		Advantages	Disadvantages
1. The branch is a fully effective unit of the firm, dealing with all local problems. 2. Often this type of unit is viewed favourably since it employs local personnel. 3. Same as 1, 2, and 3 in Direct selling (above).	1. Working within a foreign framework of laws and controls which may at times be difficult, e.g. rules regarding bringing profits home.	**Overseas branch office** (The exporter establishes an overseas branch using local personnel trained to deal with the firm's products and supervised by resident executives.)	1. Very simple from the customer's viewpoint: he appears to be dealing with a home-based company.	
1. Often very acceptably locally: offers local employment. 2. Possible tax advantages. 3. No tariff barriers.	1. Capital invested can be subject to control. 2. Profits made may be difficult to bring home. 3. Subject to local regulation in many ways.	**Overseas subsidiary company** (Subsidiary company set up in the export market.)	1. Now dealing with a home-based company. 2. No problems of import control.	

Table 1.3 (cont.)

Exporter		Channel of overseas trade (The description in brackets explains its organisation)	Overseas importer	
Advantages	Disadvantages		Advantages	Disadvantages
1. Expenses shared with other firms (or a favourable BOTB joint-venture charge only payable.) 2. The expertise of other firms (or the BOTB) is available to those new to exporting. 3. Possibility of featuring products at seminars and symposia associated with the display.	1. Limited display space (but special arrangements might be made.) 2. Fair distribution of costs essential – basis has to be agreed.	**Joint selling (joint-venture) schemes** (A group of firms co-operates in taking a stand – or organising a travelling display – to an overseas market. Under the BOTB joint-venture scheme exporters are given 15 m of space and a shell stand to display their exhibits.)	1. Opportunity to establish personal link with new exporters.	

Note: Although these are the chief types of channel open to exporters, all sorts of variations are possible to suit particular situations, and an important aspect of international trade is the flexibility of arrangements made by the most expert operators.

1.8 Commodity markets, merchants and brokers

A commodity market is a market where dealers in the basic commodities of overseas trade are in contact with one another to fix prices. The activities carried out there lie at the root of the prosperity of an advanced nation like the United Kingdom, since the huge variety of sophisticated goods in use in such a nation are made from these basic commodities. They are often called 'highly organised markets' since they have established rules and procedures for trading by recognised members who are experts in the particular commodity concerned. There is usually a recognised place of business, although business may also be conducted over the telephone in some markets. In the 'exchange' or other building only members and their authorised clerks are admitted. There is a recognised method of doing business between set times. Members of the public are not allowed on to the floor of the market, or to take part in dealings, for they would not understand the procedures, or be able to afford the quantities of commodities being sold. The behaviour of dealers is carefully watched to ensure proper conduct and some machinery exists for removing those who do not conform to the high standards required. Examples of such highly organised markets are the London Metal Exchange, the Manchester Royal Exchange, the Bradford Wool Exchange, the Fur Market and the Gold and Silver Bullion Markets. Other features of these highly organised markets are as follows.

1.8.1 *Standardised products and minimum contracts*

It helps a highly organised market if the product that is bought and sold is of standard quality, and dealers know exactly what they are buying and selling. Thus, on the Silver Bullion Market the standard product is silver of millesimal fineness 0.999, i.e. silver that is 99.9 per cent pure. Prices are quoted in pence per troy ounce. Metals can be refined until they reach the required standard, but many natural products are quite insusceptible to standardisation and have to be sold by auction after sampling. For example, tea varies not only from country to country but from bush to bush. The expert tea-taster will sample varieties and assess their quality before bidding for supplies which will blend to the quality of the product required. In order to deal in worthwhile quantities it is usual to specify a minimum contract: the minimum contract for sugar is 50 tonnes, and the minimum for copper is 25 tonnes; for barley and wheat the usual quantity is 100 tonnes and for silver it is 2,000 ounces (2 bars).

1.8.2 *Prescribed methods of dealing*

An essential feature of these markets is their competitive nature. They are the closest we can get in real life to the 'perfect competition' of economic theory. A perfectly competitive market requires that there shall be a large number of buyers and sellers dealing in standardised products who are all fully informed about prices in the market. They will therefore either buy from the cheapest supplier, or sell to the highest bidder, and in this way prices will level out at a fair price for the day.

Some markets operate with 'open outcry', buyers shouting their bids and sellers shouting their offers. It is pandemonium at busy times and there is usually a time-limit set, of, say, five minutes, for dealings in a particular commodity. In the London Metal Exchange the deals are made in the 'Ring', a circle of curved benches where the members face one another to buy and sell, with clerks standing behind them outside the 'Ring' to record the bargains and prices.

Other markets operate by private treaty, rather than open outcry, the buyer approaching sellers and asking quietly what prices and quantities they have to offer. Although obviously not as open as 'open outcry', the large number of buyers and sellers and the longer period of time allowed for these quiet negotiations makes the market just as competitive.

Auction sales, such as sales of tea, wool and other products insusceptible to standardisation, are conducted at specific times, with dealers from the countries concerned mounting the rostrum to auction the lots already sampled by the buyers. Bidding is brisk and competitive.

1.8.3 *'Futures' trading*

Trading in 'futures' is not always possible; for example the markets where sampling is necessary are usually 'spot' markets, the goods on sale being available for delivery at once – if not from the exchange, then at least from a known warehouse, stockpile, or other place of storage. The markets where products are standardised, and dealers know exactly what they are buying, may still vary in price from day to day. A bar of silver may be worth more one day than another, and over a period of three months may vary considerably. It follows that in planning production management is faced with a dilemma: it must cost its raw materials at some sort of estimated price, but does not know whether these prices will be realistic in three months' time when production actually starts. Fortunately, since there are always people oppositely placed in any production scene, it is possible to arrange firm future prices which safeguard both parties. Consider the following cases.

'A' manufactures biscuits and is proposing to lay down a production line which will require 50 tons of appropriate quality wheat a week. He has costed this at current prices and envisages a profit on the total venture as a result. He is apprehensive that prices may rise in the future and render his calculations incorrect.

'B' is a farmer planting wheat for physical delivery at a future date. He is able to meet expenses and earn a profit at current prices. He is apprehensive that the price of wheat may fall and render his activities unprofitable.

These two parties are in opposite positions: one fears a rise in price, and the other fears a fall in price. By agreeing to a futures contract at the current price they are both covered against the risk they fear. If world prices rise, B must still supply A at the old prices. A futures contract is therefore similar to insurance. If prices move either way, one of the parties will benefit from the futures contract and the other will lose out, for had he not been tied to a futures contract he might have traded at a more favourable price, and secured a windfall profit. However, with the futures contract both parties benefit to the extent that they have peace of mind, and are not gambling upon favourable prices in the future for the success of their ventures.

In fact it would probably be difficult for these two parties to come into contact with one another directly, and the futures contracts would actually be made with a broker active in the field, who is a trading member of the appropriate futures market. These intermediaries may act directly on behalf of an ultimate buyer or seller, or may act as speculators, gambling for themselves, using their expert knowledge of the trends in the market to make a profit. This means they might buy from a seller at a favourable price, hoping in due course to sell to a buyer before physical delivery takes place, so that the ultimate physical delivery will be to the buyer who actually needs the commodity for manufacture. This type of speculation thus means that risks are transferred from the seller, or the buyer, to the speculator who is prepared to carry them. Since the market has many speculators, there will always be someone to buy at a fair price for that particular day and interval of time and there will always be someone to sell at a fair price for that particular day and interval of time.

The technicalities of futures trading cannot be discussed fully here and the reader is referred to specialist texts for a full discussion of the problems.

1.8.4 *Merchants, agents, brokers and speculators*

A merchant is a wholesale trader who deals in a particular commodity or range of commodities as principal. This means that in buying the commodity he becomes the owner of it, though he may never need to take physical delivery of it, selling before delivery is due to take place to someone who actually does need the commodity.

An agent is an intermediary who arranges contracts on behalf of his principal but is not himself a party to the contract. The bargains he makes are struck between his principal and the other party, both of whom have rights and duties under the contract. In commodity markets agency arrangements are not as common as other forms of dealing, since the distance between the two parties may be very great.

A broker is a firm which buys from, or sells to, a customer for commission. Brokers may buy and sell for themselves or on behalf of clients. They must have the right to deal on the floor of the house, and consequently are sometimes called 'floor brokers'.

A dealer is a trader who operates on his own account, and for his own risk, in the market. He is a speculator, prepared to carry risk in expectation of a profit, and keeping track of market trends to discover irregularities in the market prices which will lead to profits. The elimination of price differentials as dealers adjust their positions to make marginal profits (or avoid marginal losses) gives the perfection which is desirable in the market, and establishes market prices.

1.8.5 *Clearing house facilities*

Most commodity markets have some sort of clearing house arrangement which records and guarantees all contracts registered with the clearing house. The essential features of a clearing house mechanism may be listed as follows.

(*a*) Contracts are registered with the clearing house on standard forms in accordance with the rules of the particular market concerned.
(*b*) Each party puts down a deposit which will be used to honour the bargain should prices move against either party.
(*c*) If prices move so much against a particular party that the initial deposit would be inadequate, the clearing house calls for a

'margin' to be paid in to provide further cover. This is repayable should prices recover.

(*d*) At maturity the clearing house eliminates all intermediaries who have handled the contract during the time of its currency, to decide who is finally dealing with whom. These actual parties will be engaged in the final settlement.

1.9 Multinationals

Multinational companies have a 'global-marketing' approach which aims at trading internationally through a very large number of overseas branches, or overseas subsidiary companies. They may be organised horizontally – all units doing similar work – such as where a car-rental firm operates worldwide with bases at every airport, seaport and major city; or they may be organised vertically, with firms in one country providing major sources of raw materials, others elsewhere engaged in manufacturing and others in wholesaling and retailing the manufactured product. Thus a firm might own iron ore deposits in Australia, steel works and motor car manufacturing plant in Japan and a chain of retail outlets all over the world to sell its motor vehicles. The advantages are that the multinational company achieves the economies of large-scale operation. It re-creates itself in each foreign country, producing goods in the country where costs are lowest and imposing its technical requirements upon the countries that it enters. It can press its point of view on governments, who are usually anxious to ensure that the multinational comes to their country rather than goes to a neighbouring one. It may demand a contribution to capital costs, or require that certain charges (such as local rates and taxes) are borne as a social cost by the local population benefiting from the job opportunities and other business it brings to the area. These arrangements change the pattern of international trade from a market system where free enterprise is the chief feature to an oligopolistic system in which production is carried out by a few powerful firms.

Criticism is frequently levelled at multinationals which, it is alleged, distort the domestic economies of the countries they enter, reduce the sovereignty of the national government, impose a 'cultural imperialism' upon the foreign state and bleed it of natural resources. While the accusations may be true to some extent as far as natural resources are concerned, other objections raised are less well founded. The multinational firm enters the foreign market not to change its domestic economy but to enjoy its advantages. Thus, if it enters the market because labour is cheaper than in its home country and it wishes to set up factories in a low-cost area, this is usually advantageous both for the country and its people. It often reinforces national sovereignty, supporting the status quo in an over-anxiety to rebut criticism. The self-sufficiency of nations has, in any case, been much reduced since the Second World War, with the signing of such agreements as the General Agreement on Tariffs and Trade and the according of 'associate' status to developing countries by such bodies as the European Economic Community.

The pattern of international trading may be considerably modified by the advent of the multinational firm. Many goods are no longer being traded internationally so much as moved from one part of a multinational to another. The question of taxation in a particular nation-state may become important. The multinational may ensure that goods are transferred from one country to another at prices that leave little or no profit to be taxed, or may ensure that the components which are expensive to produce and therefore less profitable are made in a country where taxation is heavy. A certain amount of national supervision of multinationals may be necessary to ensure fair play.

1.10 Ancillary services in export trade

In former times export trade was spoken of as an 'adventure', and prosperity for the adventurers, or their bankruptcy, followed the success or failure of the venture. Later it became clear that the more rational way to conduct overseas trade was to specialise in particular aspects of it. The merchant who actually owns the products being moved is still to be found, but a variety of ancillary services exists to promote the venture in the most economic way. Carriage is performed by shipowners and airlines, insurance is undertaken by underwriters, commercial risks are borne by commodity speculators, financial risks are run by bankers. Where the risks are too great for private enterprise to bear, we have government-sponsored bodies, such as the Export Credits Guarantee Department, to offer cover. All these ancillary services are again assisted by specialist firms. Thus we have consolidators and freight forwarders who make up full container loads and then break them down to individual consignments at their destination. We have a communication network to expedite documentation and advise the movement of cargoes. Overseas movements are supplemented by inland road and rail links, and finance is rationalised by specialist accepting houses and discount houses. Statistical services are at work to record the volumes and values of cargoes on the move, and customs and port authorities are monitoring them to secure the specified contributions to the national exchequer or the institutional financial machine.

The function of all these ancillary services will be made clear as this book proceeds.

1.11 Summary of Chapter 1

1. There are three major types of economy: free enterprise economies, mixed economies and controlled (communist) economies. All must engage in international trade.
2. The United Kingdom is a mixed economy, having some state-run industries and some private enterprise industries.
3. United Kingdom trade traditionally featured importation of many raw materials and foodstuffs, and the export of manufactured goods and services such as banking, transport and insurance. More recently it has included the importation of many sophisticated products which we could make ourselves, but are bound to admit under 'free trade' rules associated with membership of the European Economic Community and with the General Agreement on Tariffs and Trade.
4. There are many sources of information on overseas trade markets, both official and unofficial, with which export personnel must become familiar.
5. Export trade may be carried on through specialist export houses, which may act as merchants, agents or confirming houses. Alternatively, firms may appoint agents or set up branches or subsidiary companies abroad.
6. A sophisticated network of commodity markets exists to arrange the import of basic commodities required by industry. They frequently include a futures market where forward dealings are possible to reduce risks.
7. Multinational companies change the pattern of international trade from a market-orientated system to an oligopolistic system, where production and pricing are planned by a few powerful firms. Many international movements of goods under this system are only from one branch of the multinational to another.
8. The alert overseas trade executive must be aware of the dynamic situation in which he operates, so as to maximise profits in

favourable conditions and minimise losses when trends are adverse.

9. The ancillary services of banking, insurance, transport and physical distribution are very important in overseas trade, for they alone can ensure its successful and profitable execution.

1.12 Questions on Chapter 1

1. What are the chief features of a 'mixed economy' and a 'controlled economy'? How may they differ as far as the problems of trading with them are concerned?
2. A Yorkshire manufacturer tells you that he is thinking about opening up a market in South America for his woollen cloths. He asks you what difficulties he is likely to meet, and what channels of trade are most suitable for him. How would you advise him?
3. 'We should exclude foreign competition as much as possible to protect our own industries.' Discuss this proposition in the light of the modern situation in overseas trade.
4. Compare (*a*) overseas trade conducted with an export house with (*b*) overseas trade carried on with a subsidiary company incorporated in the market country and employing local nationals.
5. At one time merchants sat around 'waiting for their ships to come in'. Now they rarely own any ships, which tend to be run by shipowners. Why has this change come about?
6. 'When a firm sets up a foreign branch it must carry out the export activities itself – but of course it may use ancillary services.' What are ancillary services and what is their role in international trade?

Chapter 2
The balance of payments – with special reference to the United Kingdom

2.1 What is a balance of payments?

When a country engages in international trade, a special problem arises called the 'balance of payments' problem. It arises because the people of every country in the world want to be paid for the goods they make, or the services they render, in their own currency. If we want to buy American machine tools we have to pay for them in dollars, and if we want to buy Brazilian coffee we must pay for it in cruzeiros. It follows that we must obtain the dollars or the cruzeiros from someone, and the best way to do that is to sell the Americans or the Brazilians something that they want which we can offer, like Scotch whisky or insurance services. If we can sell to them exactly as much as we want to buy from them then we have a very simple balance of payments with that country.

In fact, of course, it rarely works out as easily as that. It is much more likely that we will want more from Brazil in value than they want from us, or vice versa. In such cases we cannot achieve a balance of payments. Fortunately, in most cases we can get round the difficulty by using some other currency which is acceptable to them, or by paying in gold, which is widely acceptable. It makes matters very simple indeed if we declare our own currency to be convertible, that is it can be exchanged into other currencies or into gold quite freely by an foreigner who has obtained possession of it in the course of trade.

We are still left with the point, however, that we must still achieve a total balance of payments with the other countries of the world. Otherwise – sooner or later – they will refuse to trade with us. To make this clearer we will look at the situation in diagrammatic form later in the chapter (see Figure 2.3). Meanwhile, let us pause for a moment to discuss two more expressions, bilateral trade and multilateral trade.

2.1.1 *Bilateral trade*

Bilateral trade is trade with only two sides taking part. A lot of bilateral trade agreements are made with communist countries. Having a controlled economy, communist countries find it very difficult to trade with other nations unless they have struck individual bargains with them. This is because their money system is not subject to market forces – supply and demand – but has a value set upon it by the central authorities from which it is not allowed to change. Roubles earned by a United Kingdom exporter could not be used to buy American machine tools therefore, partly because it would be difficult to find an American firm willing to take them, but also because, even if we could find a supplier prepared to take the roubles, the Russian authorities might not be prepared to let the supplier spend them on something he wanted. Another problem is that COMECON countries (belonging to the Council for Mutual Economic Co-operation) tend to buy FOB (fee on board) and sell CIF (cost, insurance and freight) so that their own shipping and insurance services are used. When buying FOB the Russian trading representatives are prepared to pay for the goods supplied and all charges necessary to get the goods to the docks or airport and on to a Russian ship or aircraft. The carriage by sea and air will be done by Russian seamen or aircrew, and insurance will be covered by Soviet state insurance schemes. When selling Russian goods they will insist that the foreign customer pays for the goods, and for their carriage and insurance. They thus do their utmost to get the best of both bargains.

There are other problems too. For example, if India sells Russia raw materials and takes manufactured goods in exchange, there is a difference in the cubic capacity required. Ships unloading a full cargo in Russian ports have hardly anything to take away on the return journey and are virtually forced to make a journey with one 'empty leg'. Bilateral trade is an unsatisfactory system of trading, for it reduces trade to the level at which the least willing partner wishes to engage. This is made clear in Figure 2.1. Since only two countries, A and B, are involved, trade will cease at £5m each way (world trade of £10m) because Country A does not want to buy more than £5m of machinery and Country B will therefore be sold only £5m of wheat.

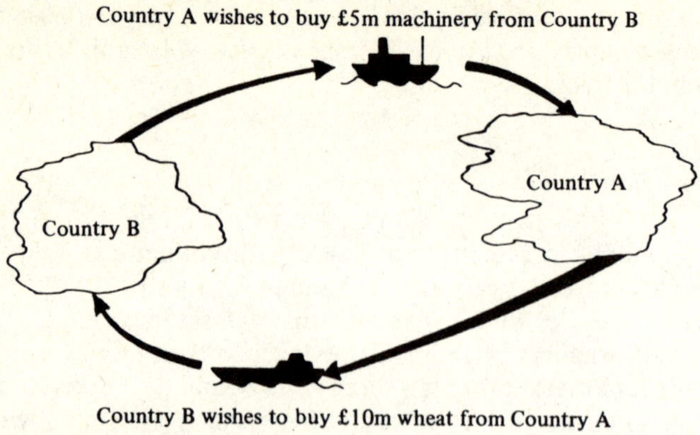

Figure 2.1 Bilateral trade – trade between only two countries.

2.1.2 *Multilateral trade*

Multilateral trade is trade where many countries are involved. It usually means a higher level of world trade if more than two nations are taking part because a country that earns a surplus of one foreign currency can spend it in other countries. This is explained in Figure 2.2. Here, since a third country is involved, world trade rises to £25m. Country A supplies £10m wheat to Country B, who pays for it with £5m machinery to Country A, and £5m machinery to Country C. Country C pays for this machinery with £5m of railway engines sent to Country A.

We can see, therefore, that multilateral trade is a more sensible and logical way to trade, since we need not balance our payments with

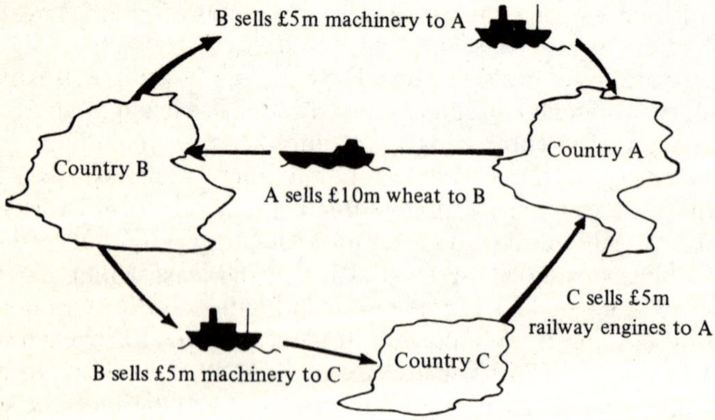

Figure 2.2 Multilateral trade – trade involving several countries.

each nation separately. Instead, we can carry on trading with other nations to any extent we like, so long as we achieve a balance of payments overall.

To conclude this section we can now define a balance of payments.

A balance of payments is a situation achieved when the total sales of a country's goods and services to other nations exactly equal the total purchases it makes of goods and services from abroad. It has three elements: the balance of trade, the balance of invisibles and the balance of capital items.

Consider illustrations (*a*) and (*b*) in Figure 2.3.

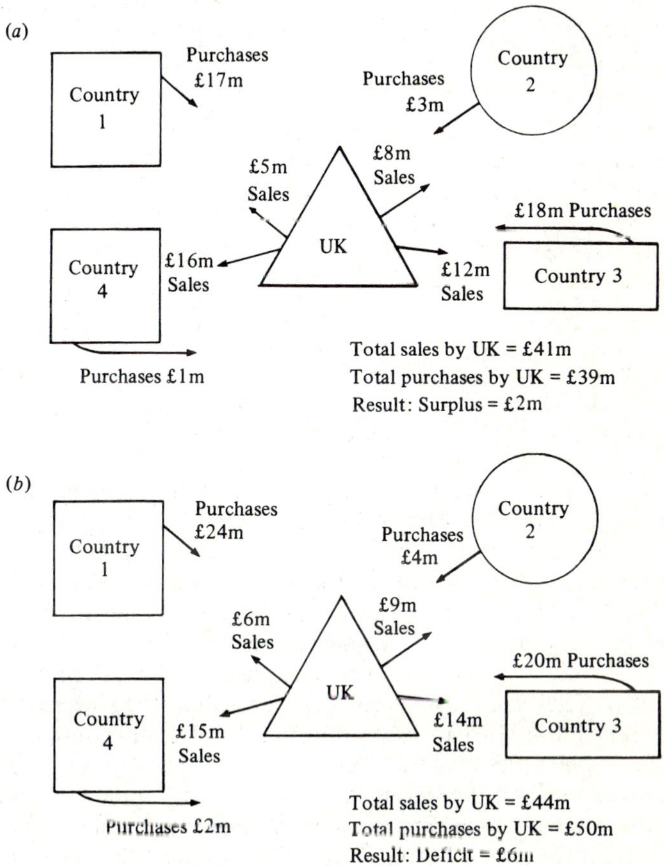

Figure 2.3 (*a*) A surplus on the balance of payments. (*b*) A deficit on the balance of payments.

These illustrate respectively a surplus on the balance of payments and a deficit on the balance of payments. Clearly, we would be very lucky indeed in any given year to find that we had purchased exactly the same amount of goods and services from abroad as we had sold to foreign nations. Every year we are sure to finish up with either a surplus or a deficit. The figures given in Table 2.1 below show the results from 1954 to 1981. A plus sign indicates a surplus, a minus sign a deficit.

Table 2.1 Balance of payments figures 1954–81 (+ = surplus; − = deficit)

Year	£ million	Year	£ million
1953	+ 296	1968	− 1,410
1954	+ 126	1969	+ 743
1955	− 229	1970	+ 1,420
1956	− 159	1971	+ 3,353
1957	+ 13	1972	− 1,141
1958	+ 290	1973	+ 210
1959	− 40	1974	− 1,646
1960	+ 293	1975	− 1,465
1961	− 339	1976	− 3,628
1962	+ 192	1977	+ 7,362
1963	− 58	1978	− 1,126
1964	− 695	1979	+ 1,905
1965	− 353	1980	+ 1,372
1966	− 591	1981	+ 6,036
1967	− 671		

Source: *The Pink Book*, 1982

The figures show clearly that our balance of payments figures fluctuate a good deal. They also show the progress of inflation. In the 1950s and 1960s deficits of a few hundred million were considered terrible, and called for massive stop–go policies. The deficit of 1964 led to a general election fought on a slogan about '13 years of Tory mis-rule'. The figures in the 1970s nearly always involved either deficits or surpluses measured in thousands of millions. The year 1977 was the year that the International Monetary Fund (IMF) was monitoring the British economy. The surplus, after several years of deficit, was staggering, but regrettably much of it was 'hot money', i.e. short-term capital movements of money flowing in to earn the high interest rates being offered by the United Kingdom. Surpluses in 1979–81 reflect the exploitation of North Sea gas and oil discoveries, rather than any real improvement in United Kingdom manufacturing industry.

2.2 A detailed look at balance of payments figures

It is convenient to look at balance of payments figures under four headings, as follows:

(*a*) 'visible' items,
(*b*) 'invisible' items,
(*c*) capital items, and
(*d*) official financing activities.

These can best be explained using actual figures. Let us look at the figures for 1981 in greater detail (see Table 2.2). Balance of payments figures are published each year in about September, giving the figures to 31 December of the previous year.

With these figures in Table 2.2 before us we can now look carefully at each section.

2.2.1 *Visible items*

Visible items are items that can actually be seen passing through our docks and airports. Wheat, oil, rubber, tin, coffee and tea are 'visible' imports, and United Kingdom cars, machinery and petrochemical products are 'visible' exports. As a country which has used up most of its raw materials (except coal) and which has a dense population and so cannot grow all its own food, we would expect to have a deficit on visible items perhaps. Indeed, in only two years since 1958 have we had a favourable balance of visible trade. In every other year we have had a loss, running as high as £5,350 million in 1974 and £3,404 million in 1979. The 1980 figures for visible trade have already been given in Table 1.1 (see page 4). Unfortunately, due to industrial action by civil servants, detailed 1981 figures are not available, but 1981 shows a favourable balance of £1,178 million. Despite the favourable balance – largely the effect of North Sea oil and gas which has reduced United Kingdom imports of foreign fuel – the situation is worrying. The balance actually earned on manufactured goods is falling year by year, and the time is fast approaching when the United Kingdom may show an adverse balance on manufactures. It is clearly undesirable that this should ever be so.

2.2.2 *Invisible items*

Invisible items are services rendered to foreigners, or services received from foreigners. The chief invisible items are banking, shipping, insurance, air transport, tourism and interest on foreign investments. In 1981 we did rather well – as we usually do – with *able 2.2* UK balance of payments, 1981

CURRENT ACCOUNT

The balance of visible trade

)ebits (debts to foreigners)	£m	Credits (debts by foreigners)	£m
Imports (valued free on board)	48,087	Exports and re-exports (valued free on board)	51,100
Favourable balance on visible trade	3,013		
	£m 51,100		£m 51,100

The balance of invisibles

			Favourable visible balance	3,013	
ayments (invisible imports)			Receipts (invisible exports)		
Government services	1,239		Government services	464	
Sea transport	3,870		Sea transport	3,772	
Civil aviation	1,922		Civil aviation	2,359	
Travel and tourism	3,285		Travel and tourism	2,999	
Financial services (*see opposite*)	–		Financial services (net of imports)	1,954	
Other services	2,463		Other services	5,206	
Interest, profits, etc.			Interest, profits, etc.		
Government	1,620		Government	940	
Non-government	7,458		Non-government	9,142	
Other transfers:			Other transfers:		
Government	3,339		Government	1,658	
Non-government	1,119		Non-government	844	
		26,315			29,338
'avourable balance on current account		6,036			
		£m 32,351			£m 32,351

'ource: The Pink Book, 1982

these invisible items and we earned far more from foreigners than they earned from us. The result is that the Current Account balance – the total of the year's activities in producing goods and services – rose to £6,036 million, of which £3,013 million was the visible surplus and £3,023 the invisible surplus. It might seem, therefore, that in 1981 we did tolerably well as a nation in the sphere of international trade in goods and services.

Table 2.2 (cont.)

Capital items

			Favourable balance on Current Account		6,036
Private sector investments in foreign firms			Foreign investment in UK		
Direct	5,157		Direct	874	
By oil companies	1,380		By oil companies	1,904	
Portfolio	4,100		Portfolio	508	
			Miscellaneous	70	
Total		10,637			
			Total foreign investment in UK		3,356
Government loans to foreigners		334	Foreign currency borrowing by banks		1,404
Export credits extended		999	Sterling borrowing by banks		2,747
External lending by UK banks		2,980	Imports credits received		115
			Other external borrowing		39
			Other transactions		80
			Allocation of SDRs		158
			Balancing item		328
			Adverse balance for official financing		687
		£m 14,950			£m 14,950

Official financing

(Monetary movements to absorb surpluses earned)

Unfavourable balance for official financing	687	Drawings from reserves	2,419
Loans to overseas monetary authorities (net)	145		
Foreign currency lending (net)	1,587		
	£m 2,419		£m 2,419

2.2.3 *Capital items*

In years gone by the capital items section of the balance of payments was a relatively small and unimportant section, consisting chiefly of loans made by the British government to Commonwealth governments abroad. It was rare for these figures to exceed £200 million. As the figures in Table 2.2 show, this is no longer the case. Thousands of millions of pounds are being juggled in innumerable flows of 'hot money'. 'Hot money' refers to money which is seeking a secure investment, at a good rate of interest. It flows from place to place, seeking security and high interest rates, and hence its name 'hot' – since the coinage metals flow most easily when they are hot. In 1981 it was still a major preoccupation of the western advanced nations to recycle the oil revenues being earned by the oil exporting countries back to replace the money being lost. This alone could prevent some countries from going bankrupt. If the money paid to the oil producers was paid back by them for western goods, or loaned by them to western industrialists in return for a fair rate of interest, economic collapse could be avoided. Also, 1981 was only the second full year since the abolition of exchange control. For the first time in 40 years United Kingdom citizens and firms have been free to invest capital in foreign countries, and consequently in 1981 capital flows were very heavy. This investment may be direct, into the establishment of foreign subsidiaries, or it may be portfolio investment, simply buying foreign stocks and shares. The item 'portfolio' on each side of the accounts shows how much was invested abroad by United Kingdom citizens and firms, compared with how much foreign capital was spent on British stocks and shares. The result of all these movements on capital account was that the favourable balance of £6,036 million on current account was turned into a deficit of £687 million. This means that the excess of capital movements out of the United Kingdom was £6,723 million, i.e. nearly £7 billion. Remember, though, that capital outflows in any one year result in revenue inflows (of interest, profits and dividends) in subsequent years, as well as capital repayments in future years. At one time the United Kingdom had huge earnings of this sort from every country in the world, and much of the prosperity of the nation arose from such earnings. The impact of these new overseas investments is a feature we might watch for in the balance of payments in the years ahead.

2.2.4 *Official financing activities*

This is the last part of the balance of payments. At the end of the year, when all the figures have been worked out, a final balance is struck. In 1981 it was a deficit of £687 million. Before we see what has to be done about this, let us just notice one further point. There is a figure in the calculation called a 'balancing item'. This is a strange figure. It is really a whole mass of errors that have been made in the calculations. The reader may feel that a figure of £328 million is a pretty big error. In fact it amounts to less than 1 per cent error. These days, with hot money flying around the world at electronic speeds, it is difficult to get exact figures at any time. Without taking this £328 million into account the deficit was £1,015 million. Yet the 'official financing' section shows that the deficit, and the loans the government was making to foreign monetary authorities of £145 million and foreign currency lending of £1,587 million, could all be financed by drawing £2,419 million from the reserves. Clearly the deficit was not as big as the figures suggested, and the errors of £328 million had to be inserted as the 'balancing item' to make the accounts balance.

It is now appropriate to return to the final problems with the balance of payments. If the country is in deficit the government (which means the Bank of England acting as the Treasury's representative) has two possible courses of action. The first is that it can pay up the deficit out of the reserves. That is what reserves are for, as every householder, who is forced to draw out his savings to pay for excessive spending, knows. Alternatively, it can arrange a loan from a foreign bank. This is like the ordinary householder who has overspent on a festive season and has to phone to ask the bank manager to sanction an overdraft.

If the country has earned a surplus, the surplus can be added to the reserves, thus increasing the nation's reserves at the Bank of England, or it can be made available as loans to foreign countries in difficulties. Naturally interest will be charged on such loans, and this will mean extra earnings for the nation in the next accounting year.

It has been said that the balance of payments always balances. It has to, or we should not be able to buy the goods we want abroad. If a day ever comes when we are unable to raise the money we need, we shall have to face up to the problem. We all read in the papers of meetings of bankers or of the International Monetary Fund, when a particular nation is in financial difficulties and cannot balance its balance of payments. The chief difficulty arises when – year after year – there is a deficit on a nation's balances and the nation must attempt to cure a permanent disequilibrium on its balance of payments.

2.3 A disequilibrium on the balance of payments

In any year the balance of payments may result in a surplus or in a deficit. If we finish up with a surplus, it means we have sold more to foreigners than we have bought from them. This means that they owe us money, and we are said to be a 'creditor' nation. Over the last few years this has happened fairly frequently, thanks to the advent of North Sea oil. Before this the United Kingdom was often in difficulties and in 1976 was in such serious difficulties that the International Monetary Fund had to be called in to help monitor the economy. The result was a massive surplus in 1977, as shown in Table 2.1. How do nations deal with such a disequilibrium?

We have seen that there are two ways, i.e. paying up out of the reserves, or borrowing from foreign banks and governments.

Most nations keep a reserve of gold and foreign currencies, rather like a prudent householder keeping a reserve in the bank for a rainy day. One way to get over a deficit is to pay up what you owe out of the reserves. If your reserves are big enough, this is no problem, and it is the best way out of the difficulty – after all, that is what reserves are for. The trouble is that the United Kingdom's reserves are not all that large, and belong partly to overseas nations like Singapore and Hong Kong, so we have to be careful not to use their reserves to settle our indebtedness.

The reserves are now revalued annually to take account of changes in the values of gold and foreign currencies. In March 1982 the United Kingdom reserves were valued as shown in Table 2.3. By contrast, in 1976 when the IMF was called in reserves had sunk to only $4,129 million.

Table 2.3 United Kingdom official reserves, March 1982

	$ million
Gold	4,546
Special Drawing Rights	1,041
Reserve position in the IMF	1,432
Convertible currencies	11,950
Total	18,969

Source: Bank of England Quarterly Bulletin

Suppose one year we have an adverse balance of payments, which we solve by paying some of it up out of our reserves and borrowing from foreign countries. Suppose that the next year we have a favourable balance. The monetary authorities breathe a sigh of relief, pay back the money borrowed the previous year (with interest) and put the rest back into the reserves to replenish them. All is well, and we are once again paying our way in the world.

Now consider what happens where we have a series of bad years.

The first year we run down our reserves and also get into debt. The next year we run our reserves even lower and get deeper in debt. The third year we have practically no reserves left and are heavily in debt to other nations. Clearly this cannot go on. We must do something about the state of permanent disequilibrium we have got ourselves into. What can we do?

The answer lies in going back to the root cause of the problem and solving it. The root cause of a disequilibrium is that we are exporting too little and importing too much. To solve the problem we must increase our exports and decrease our imports. Historically this has been done in three ways, which we will consider in turn:

(*a*) by the gold standard mechanism,
(*b*) by managed flexibility, or
(*c*) by floating (i.e. flexible) exchange rates.

2.3.1 *The gold standard mechanism*

The gold standard mechanism worked like this. All currencies, the £, the $, etc., were tied to gold and were not allowed to fluctuate in value at all. If they did – because, for example, pounds were plentiful and dollars were scarce, so that the pound fell against the dollar – then the gold standard mechanism came into effect. Pounds would become plentiful compared with dollars only if we were buying more from the USA than she was buying from us – in other words if our imports were high and our exports low. When this happened the falling value of the pound caused gold to flow out of the United Kingdom and as it left the note circulation was cut, money became scarce, business collapsed into a slump and workers were dismissed. The actual way in which this happened is fully explained in *Economics Made Simple* (for details of this text, see Chapter 9). The fact is that the gold standard mechanism solved the balance of payments problems by putting people out of work: unemployment reduced the standard of living at home and consequently reduced the demand for imports, and also for home-produced goods, which could therefore be exported. It cut wages and made our home-produced goods cheap, so that foreigners found them more attractive. The next year the balance of payments would come right, at the expense of unemployment in the United Kingdom. The United Kingdom finally left the gold standard in 1931 and for a few years used a system of floating exchange rates, to which she has recently returned. From 1944 she used the system known as 'managed flexibility'.

2.3.2 *Managed flexibility*

Managed flexibility was the system agreed at the Bretton Woods Conference in 1944, and continued until 1970. Instead of an inflexible exchange rate tied to the value of gold, it allowed the exchange rate to fluctuate a little (about 1 per cent) either side of an agreed parity with the US dollar. Thus the figure fixed in 1948 of \$2.80 = £1 allowed the £1 to fluctuate between \$2.78 and \$2.82. If fluctuations were caused by speculation – that is to say, financiers deliberately selling currency to lower its value so that they could buy it back more cheaply – this could be resisted by the use of a special fund called the Exchange Equalisation Reserve Fund. Even today we often find the phrase 'The Bank of England supported sterling actively yesterday' in our financial reports. This means that the Bank of England used the Reserve Fund to defeat speculation on the foreign exchange market. We could support sterling if it was being unfairly attacked. We could not support it if it dropped below the range \$2.82–2.78 for other reasons connected with the unsatisfactory working of the British economy – because our goods and services were not selling well enough abroad. If the pound moved outside this range, the government had to step in and take action to manage the economy by reducing the money supply, raising bank rate, hire purchase controls, etc. This meant that a certain amount of unemployment was caused, but the effects were less severe than those caused by the gold standard mechanism formerly used. The reduced demand caused by unemployment and expensive credit meant imports were less strongly demanded, wage increases were reduced and exports consequently were more competitive in world trade and more attractive to foreigners.

This type of government interference came to be called stop–go policies, and in many cases they worked quite effectively to keep the balance of payments right. However, the dislocation of these stop–go policies was strongly resented, especially by powerful trade union voices quick to blame the capitalist system for interfering with levels of employment in the interests of balance of payments equilibrium. The demand rose to put an end to this stop–go cycle, and its effectiveness was greatly reduced by such ideas as redundancy payments to staff dismissed. If the balance of payments can be corrected only by lowering the standard of living at home, then it does not help to introduce redundancy payments or other welfare schemes to raise the standard of living in bad times. If you do that the demand for imports will still be high, and the price of our exports will still be high (because the firms have to pay taxes to find the redundancy payments money).

The result of these refusals to accept stop–go policies was a succession of adverse figures on the balance of payments, and led to the use of the other solution of difficulties under the managed flexibility system. This was *devaluation*. If a country suffered from a permanent disequilibrium in its balance of payments, the Bretton Woods system said that its currency should be devalued to a new agreed figure against the dollar. Other nations would thus face more severe competition from the goods of the devaluing country, but by a gentleman's agreement they would not themselves devalue to stop this competition. In 1967 the £1 was devalued to $2.40. This was a profound shock to all those countries who had left their money with the Bank of England, for, of course, all these funds were in sterling and they lost 14 per cent of their value overnight. The sterling area was dealt a severe blow in this way, and in the next few years virtually ceased to exist.

Even this devaluation did not entirely solve the balance of payments difficulties and, since a further devaluation was not likely to be acceptable to international monetary authorities, a new system of floating exchange rates was introduced by the British government. Its effect was in the end to produce the breakdown of the managed flexibility system and a very unsettled situation in international trade.

2.3.3 *Floating exchange rates*

The problem is to reduce imports and increase exports. How can this be done without actually attacking employment levels in the United Kingdom, and forcing down the standard of living? The answer, which had been tried before between 1931 and 1939 in rather different circumstances, was to let the exchange rate float, and establish its own rate of parity under the market forces of supply and demand. The following example illustrates what happens.

(1) UK imports are considerable and many UK citizens are offering £ sterling to buy foreign goods. There are lots of pounds coming on to the foreign exchange markets.
(2) UK exports are few, because UK goods are expensive and very few foreigners are offering to buy them. There is a shortage of dollars, francs, Marks, etc., on the foreign exchange market.
(3) Clearly, under the influence of market forces of supply and demand, the exchange rate will alter. Pounds will fall against

the dollar. Instead of £1 exchanging for $2.40, it will exchange for 2.39, 2.38, 2.35, 2.25, etc. At the time of writing it is down to $1.56.

(4) This will mean that British goods get cheaper to foreigners, and more attractive. It will also mean that foreign goods get more expensive to UK citizens. So the balance of payments should be corrected, because we increase our exports and decrease our imports.

There are good reasons for thinking that floating exchange rates are a better system than fixed exchange rates, since fixed rates are bound to get out of date in time as some economies expand and others contract.

There are some side effects of this policy which are very important for international trade and which should be considered briefly.

(a) The effect on contracts made in sterling If a contract is made in sterling, the foreigner who is selling goods to the United Kingdom may find that when he actually gets paid for the goods the sterling he receives is worth less because the pound has depreciated on the foreign exchange markets. He will be rather displeased with this, and may try to get round the difficulty by using the forward exchange market. This is explained in section 3.8.1. Alternatively, he may refuse to sell goods unless the contract is specified in his own home currency or he may even go elsewhere and sell to someone else. By contrast the foreigner buying from the UK may be very happy to make the contract in sterling, and may then hold up payment as long as possible hoping that sterling will depreciate against his own currency.

(b) Retaliatory responses to floating currencies If one country floats its currency so that it depreciates under market influences, its goods will become more competitive and consequently attract foreign customers, probably diverting them from their usual markets. This may lead other nations to float their currencies to compete once again for business. The result is that nation after nation switches over to a floating currency, and the competitive edge gained by the original 'floater' is lost. Since all currencies are now floating freely – except the controlled economies – we can see what a powerful reaction there has been to the original UK 'float'.

(c) Greater uncertainty in international trade The great merit of 'managed flexibility' was that it gave reasonable certainty in

international trade. If you made a contract, you could be pretty sure you would get the price you had agreed, because the currency could fluctuate only 1 per cent (provided, of course, there was no devaluation). Since most bargains had 20 per cent or more profit element, to lose 1 per cent was not a serious loss. With floating currencies you cannot be sure what you will get, until you actually get it. Also under managed flexibility the country that was not working hard, and was inefficient, had to suffer the penalties of its own incompetence and take a cut in its standard of living to keep its balance of payments right. Under the floating exchange rates system the punishment for incompetence is not so certain and other, more conscientious, nations may suffer setbacks which are unfair.

In order to reduce these uncertainties the International Monetary Fund (described in section 2.4 below) changed its rules in 1976. Members of the Fund agreed to abide by a modified Article IV of the constitution, which requires members to pursue policies in their own domestic economies which foster orderly growth, with reasonable price stability. They undertake to avoid manipulating exchange rates to gain an unfair competitive advantage over other members (popularly known as 'beggar my neighbour policies'). At the same time a reasonable degree of management of currencies is inevitable in a free market where speculators are at work, and where those holding vast sums of a currency which is coming under pressure may be seriously affected by adverse movements in the exchange rates.

Conclusions about the balance of payments

We can draw several general conclusions about the balance of payments.

First, the balance of payments is one field where the political and administrative forces are chiefly engaged in dictating policy. This means that the government and the treasury are grappling with the problem all the time.

Second, the exporter and importer can only operate within the framework laid down by the government and the Treasury, but should act in such a way as to achieve the best possible results for themselves in the framework provided for them, which is trying to get the best results for the nation.

Third, these best results can be achieved in the long run only by dedicated work to promote the total efficiency of international trade. This degree of efficiency requires us to sell our goods, and to document, finance and transport them at the least possible cost for the best price obtainable.

It is a matter of concern to the whole nation that our exporters and importers should understand clearly the impact of their activities on the national economy.

2.4 International financial and trade organisations

There are a number of international financial and trade organisations which are influential in the export field. A brief outline is all that is possible at this point.

2.4.1 *The International Monetary Fund*

This Fund was set up after the Bretton Woods Conference in 1944, to provide a vast hoard of reserves which could be used under the managed flexibility system to give any country a bottomless pit of foreign exchange on which it could draw to resist speculation against its currency. Initially each country put a sizeable contribution into the Fund; for example, the United Kingdom's initial contribution was £1,300 million, of which one-quarter was in gold (valued at $35 per ounce) and three-quarters were in sterling. A country facing speculative pressure on its currency could come to the Fund and borrow reserves in a series of 'tranches' (the French word for slice). Each tranche was one-quarter of the value of its deposits, and up to eight tranches in all could be borrowed, i.e. double the deposit originally made by the member. Suppose sterling came under pressure. The United Kingdom would go to the IMF, borrow the first tranche – which was called the gold tranche – and return to the market to face the speculators. Any speculator selling pounds would be paid out in whatever currency he wanted (gold being freely convertible) and the Bank of England would look cheerful. If the speculation persisted, the United Kingdom would go back to the IMF for the next tranche and so on. However, as each successive tranche was borrowed the IMF would ask that the United Kingdom monetary authorities take more and more drastic steps, such as offering higher interest rates to foreign depositors, reducing home demand to cut imports, and so on. This would bring the United Kingdom economy under control. When managed flexibility was abandoned and currencies were floated freely the IMF's role was much reduced. An imbalance of payments was met by lowering the exchange rate – though a certain amount of speculation still occurs. Today the IMF is more concerned to help small nations than rescue big ones, although in some cases these amount to the same thing, for example where international bankers have loaned billions of dollars to a nation which is then unable to pay. In pursuit of a policy of demonetising gold, the Fund, by agreement, returned some gold to all nations, and sold some more at current market prices to make a huge profit which is used to aid Third World countries in financial difficulties.

One interesting feature of the IMF's work has been the creation of Special Drawing Rights (SDRs). An SDR is a paper security created by the Fund and allocated to countries on a pro rata basis, according to the size of their economies. They amount to additional reserves, which depend for their value on 'general acceptability', just like the bank notes issued by national banks in every country. A nation requiring to settle its debts may offer to pay in SDRs, and the Fund authorities will designate which country (obviously one with plenty of reserves) should accept the SDRs and replace them with an equivalent amount of its own currency for use by the member in difficulty. As world trade grows, further issues of SDRs will be made to keep world reserves in line with the trade to be financed. The SDR is also used as a unit of account. It is a currency basket, and its value is explained later (see pages 57–8).

2.4.2 *The International Bank for Reconstruction and Development (IBRD, or World Bank)*

This Bank was also set up after the Bretton Woods Conference. Its purpose is to vet and approve projects put up to it by national governments. If approved, the Bank would borrow the money to finance the project (at favourable rates of interest since it is a reputable borrower). It would then make the money available and supervise recovery of the capital as the project came on stream. Each nation commits itself to provide an agreed sum as capital for the Bank, but only 10 per cent of the guaranteed sum is actually provided; the other 90 per cent can be called if the Bank ever gets into financial difficulty.

The Bank has about £5,000 million on loan at present and has turned in recent years to sponsoring projects which will improve a developing nation's chances of progress, rather than 'prestige' projects. Many of the Bank's early projects were less helpful than intended. The largest dry dock in the world may not be as much of an asset to a poorly developed nation as a factory to turn out basic agricultural tools, which would increase its agricultural output.

2.4.3 *The General Agreement on Tariffs and Trade (GATT)*

Almost 70 nations have now become parties to this agreement, which is designed to promote trade by reducing barriers to world trade. The commonest barriers are tariffs imposed at borders on foreign goods entering a country. These tariffs raise the price of the imported articles and therefore protect the home producers from too fierce a blast of competition. Other forms of barrier are import controls, which may vary from complete embargoes (no goods allowed in) to quotas (by volume or value). A volume quota allows a certain number of goods to enter and prohibits the rest. A value quota permits a certain amount of foreign exchange to be used to import goods, but once the limit has been reached imports are suspended for the rest of the year.

Since the United States has always been very protective of its home industries, GATT began with the USA, permitting a wide variety of goods to enter its markets in return for reciprocal rights of entry accorded to its products. This enabled many countries to earn dollars, which were useful in rebuilding their economies in the post-war period. Later, two further rounds of negotiation – the 'Kennedy Round' and the 'Tokyo Round' – led to further liberalisation of trade. General negotiations were not found to be helpful, and a 'product-by-product' basis was adopted. Some of the negotiations therefore make pretty tedious reading for anyone other than a very interested expert. The trouble is that such 'free-trade' arrangements are most easily negotiated in an expanding world economy, and the recession of the late 1970s and early 1980s has led to some vocal criticism of GATT. A major complaint is against 'dumping'.

Dumping Dumping is when nations deliberately sell goods or services to foreign countries at prices far below their true cost in order to penetrate the market. They may do this from a deliberate desire to kill off competition in the home country, but more usually it is to earn foreign exchange at any price. It might seem to be a foolish policy, since the losses must be borne by their own home nationals, but they often consider it necessary. We constantly hear calls for import controls and the British shipping industry complaining loudly about unfair competition from the Russian and Chinese carrying trades. One way of avoiding dumping is by imposing an import duty on the goods entering, if it is suspected that they are being underpriced. The key guide is the price being paid by home consumers in the exporting countries for the same goods. If a foreign exporter is selling goods at prices below the price he charges at home, he is 'dumping' the goods. This is one reason why most countries insist on an export invoice in reasonable detail to show how the price is built up. If it appears to be unfair, a duty will be imposed.

2.4.4 *Free trade areas*
Free trade is easiest to promote among groups of nations of roughly similar economic situation. It gives each nation a fair chance to trade if the level of technology available and the national income per head are about the same. Whereas GATT seeks to reach agreement between all nations (and some of the most serious criticism of GATT has come from the 80 Less Developed Countries (LDCs)), members of a free trade area, such as the European Economic Community or LAFTA (the Latin American Free Trade Area) are trying to reach agreement between only eight or ten countries at most, all of whom are at roughly similar stages of development.

The European Economic Community First established on 1 January 1958 when the original six members' signatures of the Treaty of Rome took effect, the EEC has now grown to ten by the accession of the United Kingdom, Denmark and Ireland in 1973 and Greece in 1981. The features of trade within the Community are that goods produced by the member nations are in 'free circulation' within the Community and do not have to pay tariffs as they cross borders. British goods sell freely in France and vice versa. By contrast, a 'common external tariff' is raised against foreign goods entering the Community (unless earlier agreement under the GATT arrangements permits them to enter tariff-free). The lower prices have therefore provided a great incentive for intra-Community trade to grow. United Kingdom exports to the EEC rose from £3,739 million in 1973 to £20,541 million in 1980, and imports rose from £5,138 million to £20,619 million. Of course, some of this is due to inflation rather than growth of trade, but as a percentage of total trade exports to the EEC rose from 31 per cent of total United Kingdom exports in 1973 to 43 per cent in 1980, and imports rose in the same period from 36 per cent to 42 per cent of total United Kingdom imports.

Trading with COMECON countries
International trade would be greatly boosted if a formal agreement on general trading arrangements could be concluded between the COMECON countries and bodies such as the EEC which inevitably trade with many of them. Unfortunately, there are political reasons why this cannot be arranged. First, the COMECON countries are not an economic community in the same way as the EEC, with a right to negotiate on behalf of its members. The acronym COMECON stands for Council for Mutual Economic Co-

operation, and it has no integrating structure like the European Economic Community. It tends to be dominated by the USSR and a formal agreement on trade might be seen as reinforcing the Soviet Union's right to dominate the other Eastern Bloc states.

Instead, a policy of trade liberalisation with individual nations is being pursued. Once again, as with all such negotiations, it is found to be easier to reach agreement on a product-by-product basis rather than in general terms. For example, in 1980 negotiations with Rumania led to the removal of quantitative import controls on a large range of chemical products. Import controls on many other products were either eased or, in some cases, suspended and replaced by 'voluntary restraint' agreements. Joint venture arrangements may also assist trade; for example, an agreement to proceed with the construction of power dams whose output will be shared is clearly the sort of arrangement that would benefit several parties.

One of the difficulties that arises in trade with COMECON countries concerns credit and repayment: frequently trade can proceed only if the Communist country is able to arrange credit facilities, but in many cases the repayment of these loans and the interest that accrues on them later proves impossible. Trade cannot flourish in situations where payment is uncertain.

2.5 Compensation trade or barter

A particular form of trade which is a feature of trade with COMECON and Less Developed Countries (LDCs) is *compensation trade*, or *barter*. The trading is outside normal financial arrangements, since one of the parties (or possibly both) has difficulties in finding the necessary foreign exchange. An export of one class of goods is therefore compensated by the supply of another class of goods. This is clearly easiest to arrange if the values of the two classes of goods are the same (*balanced barter*). Sometimes the value can be equalised if a third nation participates (*triangular barter*). Thus, if Country A supplies £10 million of Good X to Country B, which supplies £5 million of Good Y in compensation, plus a further £5 million of Good Y to Country C, which compensates for this by supplying £5 million of Good Z to Country A, all parties have been compensated for their exports by goods of an equivalent value. No foreign exchange has been required. Obviously, with all barter transactions each participating country must want the goods that the other has to offer and be able to offer what the other wants. A class of speculators – barter and switch operators – prepared to dabble in such arrangements does exist, but it is clearly a highly specialised field.

2.6 Summary of Chapter 2

1. The balance of payments problem is one of attempting to earn as much from our exports of goods and services as we need to buy the imports which are essential to our prosperity and way of life.
2. A balance of payments is more easily achieved in a multilateral trade situation than in bilateral trade.
3. Three aspects of the balance of payments are 'visible trade' in goods, 'invisible trade' in services, and capital movements involving long-term loans or investments. A fourth aspect, 'official financing', concerns the official activities of national governments and treasuries to finance deficits or deal with surpluses resulting from an imbalance of trade.
4. Imbalances of trade can be corrected by only three methods. These are (*a*) the gold standard mechanism, (*b*) managed flexibility (the Bretton Woods System), and (*c*) floating exchange rates. These corrective measures are distinct from 'financing', which merely carries the balances over to the next year.
5. Floating exchange rates – the prevailing method of solving balance of payments difficulties – hampers international trade by making payments less certain, though it may reflect a more realistic view of the world's economic affairs than the previous system of fixed exchange rates.
6. Certain international institutions exist to assist nations with balance of payments difficulties. The most important of these is the International Monetary Fund.
7. The General Agreement on Tariffs and Trade is an agreement by which member nations agree to reduce tariff barriers to promote free trade.
8. Free trade areas are associations of states, usually all of a similar level of economic development, between which goods are free to cross borders without the payment of tariffs. They may erect a common external tariff against goods from non-member states.
9. Compensation trade (barter) is a feature of trade with Communist and Third World countries. Exports are compensated by imports of goods to a similar value, and foreign exchange is not involved.

2.7 Questions on Chapter 2

1. Define the term 'balance of payments'. What elements are found in any balance of payments on international trade?
2. What are 'visible trade' and 'invisible trade'? How may exports of 'visibles' and 'invisibles' be increased?
3. 'The balance of UK visible trade rarely balances; the balance of UK visibles and invisibles frequently balances; the balance of payments must balance.' Explain.
4. What impact on the balance of payments does the floating exchange rate have? Explain clearly how it works towards achieving a proper balance.
5. 'Floating exchange rates have serious side effects on international trade.' Explain what these side effects are.
6. What is a free trade area? What has been the impact on United Kingdom trade of accession to the European Economic Community?
7. What is compensation trade? Distinguish between balanced barter and triangular barter.

Chapter 3
Export and import prices and terms of sale

3.1 The problem of pricing exports

Overseas trade requires particularly careful pricing if it is to be carried on profitably. It is more susceptible to interferences than inland trade, passing as it must through bottlenecks at the ports and airports. Dislocations due to accidents, bad weather, strikes, etc., can add large costs to the undertaking, while currency fluctuations can vary the actual payment received. The atmosphere in which overseas trade is carried on is charged with potential conflict, and even the terms used have different meanings in different countries. For these reasons it is necessary to proceed cautiously, to choose the wording of documents carefully, to define terms wherever possible and to build in safeguarding clauses. Even major international companies have gone out of business because fixed-price contracts for long-term supplies have been unrealistic in the light of inflationary developments.

A manufacturer or merchant selling abroad hopes to achieve a return on capital invested at least as good as he would receive from home sales. If he performs extra services, such as packaging, transport and insurance, he must charge to recoup the cost of these services, and secure a profit on any capital tied up in their performance. From the nation's point of view it is highly desirable that he should perform the fullest services possible, thus providing work for United Kingdom seamen, lorry drivers, bankers, insurance underwriters, etc. The addition of invisible exports to the value of the 'visible' goods sold is very advantageous, but this is sometimes rendered impossible because the foreign buyer is anxious to use his own merchant fleet or banking facilities, for example. Where a full service through to destination can be provided it is desirable that it should be offered.

The problem of pricing exports may therefore be divided up into four parts.

(*a*) What is the home price of the goods?
(*b*) What extra costs are being incurred in this particular export activity? This depends upon the *terms of sale* which decide the extent of the exporter's activities in every case. These are explained below.
(*c*) Are there any uncertainties which cannot be insured against? The profit margin to be added must contain an element to cover these uncertainties.
(*d*) Are there any other special considerations involved?

Each of these parts will be considered in turn.

3.2 The home price of the goods

The home price of the goods is arrived at by following well-known principles lying in the field of cost accounting, which holds that costs may be divided into two chief parts, *direct costs* and *indirect costs*.

Direct costs are those costs which can easily be attributed directly to a particular project or line of goods. Thus, the raw materials used, the wages of employees directly involved, the power directly attributable to running the machines used are all direct costs. Since they vary with the total output of this particular product, they are often called *variable costs*.

Other costs cannot be directly attributed to a particular product. These indirect costs, such as rent, rates, lighting, heating, repairs to premises, etc., have still been incurred for the purpose of pursuing the general enterprise. Every product or project must therefore contribute something towards the coverage of these costs, which are often called *fixed costs*, *invariable costs* or *overheads*. They must be allocated to each product on some fair basis.

A typical cost sheet for a particular product might therefore look something like that shown in Table 3.1.

The 'ex works' price gives the firm a reasonable coverage of the costs involved in earning the profit, and a recognised scale of profit for that particular class of goods in that particular industry.

Before going on to discuss the export price, we need to consider the terms of sale that may be arranged and the export duties (and rights) that each of these involves.

Table 3.1 A sample cost sheet

Mark II Electric Pump			
Direct costs			
			£
Raw materials			–
Tool room wages			–
Machine shop wages			–
Assembly shop wages			–
Direct power			–
		Total	–
Overheads			
Purchases dept.	–		
Goods inwards	–		
Drawing office	–		
Progress chasing	–		
Factory office	–		
Inspection	–		
Accounts	–		
Personnel	–		
Advertising	–		
Sales	–		
R & D	–		
General	–		
		Sub-total	–
		Total cost	–
Mark-up for profit			–
'Ex works' price			–

3.3 Terms of sale

There are a great many standard terms of sale in current use. They range from 'ex works' at one end of the scale to 'delivered duty paid' at the other. To overcome the difficulties which arose when terms of sale had different meanings in different countries, the International Chamber of Commerce published an agreed set of definitions called Incoterms (an abbreviation of 'international commercial terms') and the current edition is *Incoterms 1980*. An abbreviated description of the 14 terms in *Incoterms 1980* is given in Table 3.2, but students are strongly advised to purchase their own copies of *Guide to Incoterms*, which gives not only a written but also a pictorial account of the terms, with the rights and duties of each party. No office should be without its copy of this helpful guide.

Table 3.2 The terms of trade (Incoterms 1980)

Code	Name	Explanatory notes
1. EXW	Ex works	The seller's only responsibility is to make the goods available at his works or factory. The buyer bears the costs and the risks from that point on, including loading on to the vehicle (unless otherwise agreed), and the entire transit to destination. 'Ex works' terms are therefore the minimum obligation for the seller and the maximum obligation for the buyer.
2. FRC	Free carrier . . . named point	The seller is responsible for delivering the goods to a carrier – usually a multi-modal transport operator – at a named point. This could be the seller's premises, or the road haulier's premises or the railway station, etc. The risks of damage or loss pass to the buyer at that time.
3. FOR/FOT	Free on rail/ Free on truck	The word 'truck' refers to a railway wagon, so this is purely a rail term. The risk passes when the goods are handed into the custody of the railway, or are placed on board a railway wagon for transit.
4. FOA	Free on board at airport	The risks pass at the moment when the goods are handed into the custody of the air carrier at the airport of departure. From that time the risk lies with the buyer.
5. FAS	Free alongside ship	The seller's obligations cease when the goods are placed alongside the ship on the quayside, or in lighters. The buyer bears all the costs and risks of loss or damage from that moment, and even the responsibility of clearing the goods for export.
6. FOB	Free on board	The seller is responsible as far as loading the goods on board ship at the port of departure. The risk passes as goods cross the ship's rail. The buyer bears the loss if they fall upon the deck.
7. CFR	Cost and freight (formerly **C and F**)	The seller must pay the costs and the freight (freight is the carrier's reward for carrying) as far as the port of destination, but the *risk* passes to the buyer as the goods cross the ship's rail in the port of shipment.
8. CIF	Cost, insurance and freight	The seller is in the same position as in **CFR** but in addition has to provide marine insurance during the carriage. The risk passes to the buyer as the goods cross the ship's rail, and the insurance policy then covers the buyer's risk.

Table 3.2 (*cont.*)

Code	Name	Explanatory notes
9. DCP	Freight or carriage paid . . .	The seller pays the freight or carriage to the named destination, but the *risk* passes to the buyer once the goods are delivered to the first carrier, whatever the form of transport used, or the multi-modal nature of the transit. (The D in the 3-letter code may be taken to stand for 'delivered'.)
10. CIP	Carriage and insurance paid to . . .	The same as **DCP** but the seller also has to insure the goods for all modes of transport to destination. The risk transfers to the buyer when the goods are given into the custody of the first carrier, and the buyer then has the cover of the insurance policy.
11. EXS	Ex ship	The seller bears all the costs and risks of bringing the goods to the port of destination, where they are passed to the buyer. The buyer runs the risk when unloading and in the onward transit to destination.
12. EXQ	Ex quay (duty paid *or* duty for buyer's account)	The seller bears all the costs and risks until the goods are on the quay at destination. These include customs duty payable on entry to the buyer's country, unless otherwise specified. The buyer takes delivery, and assumes the risks there.
13. DAF	Delivered at frontier	The seller bears all the costs and all the risks until the goods arrive at the named frontier, but before they go through the 'customs border'. The buyer clears the goods through the import frontier, paying the duty (if any) and bearing the risks.
14. DDP	Delivered duty paid	This is the maximum commitment for the seller, and the minimum for the buyer. The seller delivers to the buyer after paying the duty on import to the country of destination. However, it is possible to deliver 'DDP exclusive of VAT and/or taxes'. The term '*franco domicile*' is now obsolete.

3.3.1 *Incoterms 1980*

There are 14 possible terms of sale laid down in the internationally agreed *Incoterms 1980*. They are shorthand expressions, each symbolised by a recognised three-letter code, which set out the agreed rights and obligations of parties concerned with the transit of goods. By studying the definitions it is possible to see who is bearing the costs and carrying the risks at each part of the transit. Should any loss occur at any particular part of the journey, the one carrying the risks at that time must bear the loss. The abbreviated definitions in Table 3.2 should make it possible to follow the transfer of risk from one party to another. Note that the explanations given are only introductory. *Guide to Incoterms* includes many helpful 'comments on the Rules'.

Whatever the terms of sale – and we have seen these range from 'ex works' at one end of the scale to 'delivered duty paid' at the other – someone will be arranging insurance cover for the goods in transit. The arrangements made will vary with the agreed terms of sale, and will reflect the passing of the insurable interest from one party to another. Where a single policy covers the entire transit on a warehouse-to-warehouse basis, the policy being assigned to the buyer, the person entitled to claim will be the one who had the insurable interest at the time the loss occurred. The point where insurable interest passes from one person to another is therefore of great importance.

If a manufacturer quotes a price 'ex works', it means that he is giving the price of the required article as it emerges from his own works entrance, with nothing but its primary packaging. From that point on, all packaging, transport, loading, unloading, freight and insurance will be for the account of the purchaser. Clearly this is a very unhelpful form of quotation, and places serious burdens upon a foreign customer. However, it is quite frequently used where an export house is acting as a confirming house and buying on behalf of its overseas client intending to see to the collection, packaging and dispatch of the article. Where a sophisticated product has to be examined, tested and certified by independent assessors before being shipped, it would clearly be a waste of time to package it anyway.

With 'delivered duty paid', by contrast, the exporter has to bear the expense of all the activities required to get the product to the importer. Thus there will obviously need to be a considerable difference between the 'ex works' price and the 'delivered duty paid' price.

Figure 3.1 illustrates the standard terms in common use, showing them from the 'ex works' price to the 'delivered duty paid' price. It is difficult in any diagram to include all the possible terms of sale or mention all the expenses which may be incurred in a particular stage of activity. For these reasons the terms DCP (delivered freight or

	Terms of sale	*Prices quoted*	£	
		Direct costs	£ –	
		+ Overhead	–	
		+ Profit	–	
EXW	Ex works	**Ex works price**	£ –	
		+ Transport (if any)	–	
FRC	Free carrier	**FRC price**		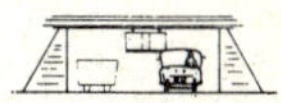
	or	or		
FOR/FOT	Free on rail/truck	**FOR/FOT price**		
	or	or		
FOA	Free on board at airport	**FOA price**	£ –	
		+ Transport to port	–	
		+ Documentation charges	–	
		+ Insurance charges	–	
FAS	Free alongside ship	**FAS price**	£ –	
		+ Dock charges	–	
		+ Stevedoring charges	–	
		+ Cranage	–	
FOB	Free on board	**FOB price**	£ –	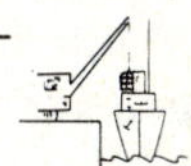
		+ Freight	–	
CFR	Cost and freight	**CFR price**	£ –	
		+ Insurance	–	
CIF	Cost, insurance and freight	**CIF price**	£ –	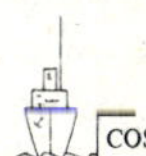
		+ Cranage	–	
EXQ	Ex quay	**Ex quay price**	£ –	
		+ Foreign port dues	–	
		+ Import charges	–	
		+ Warehousing	–	
		+ Transport	–	
		+ Costs of financial collection	–	
		+ Agency overheads	–	
DDP	Delivered duty paid	**DDP price**	£ –	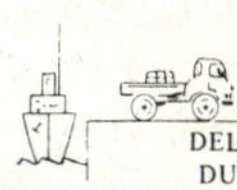

Figure 3.1 Terms of sale and their impact on quoted prices.

carriage paid to), CIP (carriage and insurance paid to), EXS (ex ship) and DAF (delivered at frontier) are not shown in the diagram.

3.3.2 *Conclusion about terms of sale*

Finally, a word should be said about the marketing aspect of terms of sale and the ability to offer a certain degree of service. It depends upon the customer, of course, but some orders will definitely be lost if the correct terms of sale are not offered. 'Ex works' terms may give a minimum of worries and responsibilities to the exporter, but a buyer who is quite unable to organise the exporting activities himself from his remote location will simply go elsewhere. It is therefore important to offer a degree of service, even if the contract is concluded based on the 'ex works' price and the exporting activities are carried out for the buyer's account.

3.4 The export price

We can now see that the price charged for an export consignment depends upon the costs of manufacture and the agreed terms of sale. According to the terms of sale the exporter must provide a degree of service. The extent of this service either is generally recognised because of internationally accepted definitions of the terms of sale, or is mutually recognised by a specific clause in the contract outlining the meaning understood for this particular contract. Despite the detailed nature of these calculations, an experienced exporter can refer to charts of charges and mark-ups and give an approximate price without hesitation. Once the terms of sale have been agreed, the price should remain fixed, and in non-inflationary times and times when exchange rates were fixed this would have been so. However, today's fluctuating exchange rates and general inflationary situation have made fixed prices very hazardous.

It is therefore becoming more usual to reserve certain rights to alter quotations in certain circumstances, for example by the insertion of a clause 'The prices quoted are based upon a world price of sugar of £*x* per ton and of wheat of £*y* per bushel. We reserve the right to adjust the quotation for any rise in these prices in excess of 2 per cent.' Similarly, 'The price CIF Baltimore is based on a freight rate of $6.75 per ton. Any variation in this rate is for buyer's account.'

Here again we have a marketing influence at work on the decisions whether or not to include variation clauses. A salesman will always be inclined to clinch an order even if there is the possibility of difficulties in the future. Often his commission depends upon the size of the order. His natural tendency is supported by the buyer's inclination to prefer a firm arrangement at a fixed price. In some notable cases bankruptcies on a spectacular scale have followed the conclusion of such 'fixed-price' contracts. If the general outlook is inflationary, or if the price of raw materials is volatile, or if freight rates form a high proportion of the total value and are known to be unstable, then it is essential to build in variation clauses, which should be precisely worded and insusceptible to misinterpretation.

Finally, it is sometimes the case that a slip is made in an export quotation, and an alert customer might take advantage of this by a prompt acceptance. A safeguarding clause, such as 'This quotation is subject to our final confirmation of your acceptance', provides for this possibility and permits revision of the offer even at such a late stage.

3.5 Import prices

Having described the price structure of exports, it is clear that the price structure of imports must be the same but in reverse. Those who have worked in importing firms develop a kindred feeling for their customers when they transfer to export employment, for they have experienced international trade from the opposite point of view.

Once again it is beneficial to the nation if goods can be carried by British ships or aircraft, insured with British underwriters and financed by British banking services. An importer buying FOB has the opportunity to find his own carrier and insurer, etc. Whether he will be able to obtain the goods he wants on these terms depends upon the anxiety of his overseas supplier to secure the order. Where the goods are in strong demand, and alternative customers are available, the UK importer may have to agree to purchase CIF.

The final price of the imported goods to the consumer will, of course, include manufacturing cost, insurance, freight, warehousing and transport costs. It will also include import duty, and Value Added Tax, as well as the profit margin required by the importer.

3.6 Terms of payment

When selling to overseas customers it is essential to safeguard oneself against the risks of overseas trade. These include not only the physical risks of loss, damage or delay in transit but other risks of non-payment, *force majeure*, conflict of laws, etc. In order to reduce such risks to the minimum it is necessary to make one's terms of sale absolutely clear, and train all staff to appreciate the danger that can follow failure to adhere to guidelines on such matters as delivery dates, methods of payment and discounts for bulk supplies.

Terms of payment range from *cash with order* at one end to *open account* at the other. Listing them in the order of least risk for the exporter we have:

(*a*) cash with order,
(*b*) documentary credits,
(*c*) documents against payment,
(*d*) documents against acceptance, and
(*e*) open account terms.

The features of these terms of payment are explained in Chapter 4.

3.7 In which currency shall the contract be expressed?

In former times contracts were invariably made in sterling, the value of which never changed. From 1745 to 1945 the rate of interest earned on sterling was roughly 2.5 per cent – a period of 200 years without any sort of inflation. Today the value of sterling varies from minute to minute, and a good deal of uncertainty has crept into international trade as a result. Not only sterling, but all currencies are floating. It follows that businessmen cannot command that their contracts are made in sterling; indeed, they might positively prefer that they are not. Contracts may therefore be made in sterling or a foreign currency, or they may be made in a 'currency basket'. This clever idea is explained below. Whatever the currency unit stated in the contract, the services of the banks and foreign exchange market are such that no real difficulty need be encountered. They can deal with any currency simply and straightforwardly and the generally recognised 'currency baskets' are easily settled in any settlement currency at the exchange rate prevailing on the day of settlement.

The point about specifying a particular currency is that if it is unstable an element of uncertainty is introduced into the contract which may render it less profitable than was hoped. Thus, if the contract (total value £45,000) is specified in sterling, and sterling depreciates in value, the money, when it comes to be paid, will still be £45,000, but it will be worth less than before. For example, a Ghanaian buying British goods for £45,000 at a time when the rates of exchange are stable at £1 = 2.60 cedis would need to pay 117,000 cedis for the £45,000 sterling he requires. At times when sterling was declining in value, say to £1 = 2.40 cedis (note that as the £1 declines in value less cedis have to be given for each £1), the Ghanaian would need to provide only 108,000 cedis to purchase £45,000 in sterling. The United Kingdom exporter would therefore receive his contract price, but it would be worth less in terms of purchasing power in the real world. Had the contract been made in cedis, the Ghanaian importer would have had to pay the full 117,000 cedis, which would on conversion have fetched £48,750 sterling. It is clear that the importer benefits and the exporter loses when a designated currency depreciates. If the designated currency appreciates, the exporter gains and the importer loses.

These difficulties can be overcome to some extent by forward dealings on the foreign exchange market, and in other ways which are outlined in section 3.8.

The next stage is to decide the currency in which the contract will be expressed. The possibilities are as follows.

(*a*) In sterling.
(*b*) In the foreign currency of the importer. Some currencies fluctuate so wildly that they are not quoted on the foreign exchange markets and so the use of this currency may not always prove to be a viable possibility.
(*c*) In a recognised neutral currency of relatively stable value, such as US dollars.
(*d*) In a currency basket.

The fourth of these possibilities, *currency baskets*, provide a way of minimising exchange risks by quoting contract prices in an 'international unit of account' made up of a currency cocktail. One of these, the European Currency Unit (ECU), is composed as shown in Table 3.3. Another is the Special Drawing Right (SDR) unit, whose composition is shown in Table 3.4.

Table 3.3 The European Currency Unit (ECU)

Currency	Weight (total = 100)	Amount in units of each designated currency
Deutsche Mark	33	0.828
Pound sterling	13	0.0885
French franc	20	1.15
Italian lira	10	109
Dutch guilder	10	0.286
Belgian franc	10	3.66
Luxembourg franc	(linked to Bfr)	0.14
Danish krone	3	0.217
Irish punt	1	0.00759

The advantage of currency baskets is that the value of the unit remains relatively stable whatever may happen to a particular currency. Thus a business which quotes its contract price in sterling runs the risk that if sterling falls in value the ultimate payment may be less than expected. If sterling falls, the values of the ECU and the SDR units will also fall, but by much less because they have only a very small amount of sterling in the 'basket' that makes up each unit. Not only this, but if sterling falls the other currencies will rise, and the rise in the currencies will offset the fall in sterling. These units are therefore relatively stable, and prices quoted in them will bring in the 'correct' amount of the settlement currency in due course. For example, if the relative settlement currency is sterling, and sterling has fallen since the bargain was struck, the agreed contract price will now be worth more sterling than before. The *increased* quantity of a *depreciated* currency leaves the businessman receiving a 'fair' price for his goods.

Table 3.4 The Special Drawing Rights unit

Currency	Weight (total = 100)	Amount in units of each designated currency
US dollar	42	0.54
Deutsche Mark	19	0.46
Pound sterling	13	0.071
French franc	13	0.74
Japanese yen	13	34

Before a final decision about the currency to be used is made, the following points should be considered.

(*a*) Predictions about the likely future strengths of alternative currencies and currency baskets, and the position at settlement day must be made.
(*b*) If finance is required, the prevailing rates of interest for sterling and alternative currencies for the time interval envisaged may affect the decision.
(*c*) The views of the foreign importer as to the currency to be specified may be important. Sales volume may be reduced if the currency is one which the foreign importer cannot obtain, or which he considers too expensive.
(*d*) Leads and lags may influence the decision. If a foreign importer has to pay in a currency which is rising in value he is likely to pay quickly (to lead with his payment). If the settlement currency is falling in value, he may lag behind with his payment, hoping it will fall even further and reduce the amount he may need to pay. To counter this the exporter may reduce credit periods when the settlement currency is expected to fall in value, and

allow extended credit periods when the currency is expected to rise in value.

3.8 Avoiding exchange risks

The exporter who has made a profitable arrangement with a foreign customer to be settled at a future date runs the risk that some of his profits will be eroded by foreign exchange movements before the agreed settlement date. Of course, it is equally possible that the exchange movements will be favourable and lead to a windfall profit, but it is no part of an exporter's activities to speculate on foreign exchange movements. The basic rule in business is to behave prudently, safeguarding what has been achieved by ordinary activities and leaving speculation to those who understand the business. It is therefore advisable to cover exchange risks either by asking a banker to arrange a forward exchange deal or a loan on the Eurocurrency market, or by making certain exchange rate stipulations in the contract.

3.8.1 *Forward contracts*

A currency which is expected to rise in the months ahead will be quoted on the foreign exchange market at a premium. The exporter may therefore be able to sell the foreign exchange due to him under the contract at a firm price now in excess of the spot price prevailing at present. This will increase the yield he will obtain from his exporting activities while at the same time eliminating any exchange risk.

Suppose an exporter contracts to sell a machine for $22,000, payable in three months' time to an American customer. The spot rate for dollars is £1 = $2.00 so that the exporter can expect to receive £11,000. On the forward exchange market the quotation for dollars three months forward is 0.85 cents premium. The dollar is expected to rise by almost 1 cent in the next three months. By selling the exchange he is due to receive forward at $1.9915, i.e. a premium of 0.85 cents, the exporter is insulated from future exchange rate fluctuations while at the same time increasing his earnings from £11,000 to £11,046.95.

3.8.2 *Eurocurrency dealings*

An alternative method of avoiding foreign exchange risks is to arrange a loan in the designated foreign currency that can be sold immediately on the spot market for the spot price. This avoids any risk of exchange loss, since the arrival of the foreign exchange in due course can be used to settle the loan. There is, of course, the risk that the foreign buyer may not pay. The loan would therefore have to be settled by the purchase of foreign currency at the spot price at the settlement date, which would mean that an exchange loss would be experienced if the foreign currency depreciated in the mean time.

3.8.3 *Contractual stipulations*

It is possible to contract in such a way that an agreed exchange rate against sterling is stipulated. Nothing that happens to the exchange rate will affect the amount payable so that an invoice price expressed in a foreign currency is known to be the equivalent of a given amount of sterling. The exchange risk is therefore borne by the foreign customer, but he would get the benefit of any favourable change in the exchange rate.

3.8.4 *LIFFE*

The London International Financial Futures Exchange was established in September 1982. This is a futures market covering a wide range of financial instruments where those expecting future receipts or payments can obtain firm prices now for future dealings. As with all futures markets it does not mean that a trader can secure spot prices now for a future date, because the spot price will naturally be adjusted by the dealers to take account of the trends they envisage. The prices quoted may therefore be at a premium, or a discount, on current prices. Although this market represents an advance in the sophisticated network of future dealings available in London, it is unlikely to be of immediate interest to exporters, who will continue to ask their bankers to secure forward cover for them in the usual ways outlined above. It is the financial institutions themselves who will use LIFFE to reduce the risks they are carrying, by narrowing the range of fluctuations they are likely to meet on the open market. The minimum contract for sterling on the currency markets of LIFFE is £25,000, while the minimum for sterling on the Sterling Deposit Market is £250,000.

3.9 Credit management

Credit management is an integral part of exporting, as it is of home business. We must limit our risks by prudent behaviour at all times, and cover ourselves by insuring against default wherever possible.

The exporter should behave prudently from the time of the first inquiry from an overseas customer (except where cash-with-order terms are required). There is little point in pursuing an inquiry if the potential customer is not creditworthy and so it is worth seeking status reports. These can be obtained almost immediately from such international credit agencies as Dun & Bradstreet Limited of London. Priority enquiries can be made by either 'one-way' or 'two-way' priority services. A one-way priority involves the credit agency calling by telex for a status report which is returned by airmail; a two-way priority service returns the status report by telex, and follows this with a full report sent by airmail. A satellite link to the USA returns status reports on American customers within three hours; European status reports can be requested direct by telex or telephone. A business traveller on a sales trip abroad can be provided with an 'International Service Card' which enables him to visit foreign branches of the credit agency for status reports. A written report is then sent to the traveller's own office. Another service is the 'Special Report' service, which is an in-depth investigation of a potential customer drawn up to meet a brief by the exporter considering a major decision involving a heavy commitment to a foreign customer's requirements.

The organisation of a worldwide credit agency is naturally a tremendous task. It requires not only routine searches of company files, but also personal assessment of the proprietors or directors of firms, and the collection of the views of each firm's principal suppliers with experience of past payment records. These data are then distilled into a credit rating which reveals how much credit it is advisable to extend to the customer concerned. This exercise can be much more satisfactory than an enquiry to a bank, which has limited facilities for conducting such investigations and which can comment only on its own personal knowledge of the customer.

Time is often of the essence in credit control. For example, goods delivered to the premises of a firm which has just gone into liquidation come under the liquidator's control and the supplier becomes a creditor entitled to sue in the bankruptcy. Deliveries should obviously be stopped, in transit if necessary, in such circumstances. *Stubbs Gazette* give a weekly account of all mortgages, charges, litigations, liquidations and bankruptcies to provide early warning of companies facing difficulty.

Trade indemnity credit insurance

Many exporters do not realise that insurance cover can be obtained for failure to pay by the buyer. In export trade the risks are higher than in home trade, since language, customs of trade, regulations and currency may all be different. There is usually a requirement that prudence has been displayed in checking the status of a customer with a reliable credit reference agency and, to spread risks as widely as possible, 'whole turnover' cover is required. The exporter insures all shipments, not just the ones considered most risky. Protection is available from the date of dispatch, and pre-delivery protection can be provided if specialised plant has been purchased or work-in-progress is particularly valuable. Transactions in foreign currencies may be covered, and insurance policies may be assigned to bankers or finance houses who are naturally more willing to provide finance if the eventual payment is covered against default. One firm offering such cover is Trade Indemnity PLC, 12–34 Great Eastern Street, London EC2A 3AX.

3.10 Summary of Chapter 3

1. Export prices and import prices can be crucial to profitability, since they are arranged in trading areas where conflicts of understanding easily arise about the exact meaning of terms of delivery and terms of payment. Since time is needed to fulfil the contracts, exchange fluctuations and other price movements can also affect the eventual financial return. If prices of raw materials, freight rates, etc., change in this period, a contract may prove unprofitable.
2. A basic element in export and import prices is the cost of production in the country of origin.
3. Terms of sale form an important element in all contracts for international trade. They decide the obligations and rights of the parties involved and specify when the property passes and risks transfer from one party to the other. The terms of sale range from 'ex works', involving very little responsibility on the part of the exporter, to 'delivered duty paid', where the exporter is responsible for all stages of the transaction up to and including the delivery of goods.
4. Export prices vary with the costs of production and the agreed terms of sale. In inflationary times it is wise, especially with long-term contracts, to insert clauses entitling the exporter to adjust prices in line with inflation.
5. Import prices are determined in the same way as export prices but must be regarded from the opposite point of view. They should also be scrutinised to detect 'dumping'.
6. Currency baskets (or currency cocktails) provide a way of reducing currency fluctuations by using international 'units of account'. The two most important currency baskets are the

European Currency Unit (ECU) and the Special Drawing Right (SDR) units.

7. Exchange risks may be avoided by forward dealings on the foreign exchange market, or by obtaining an immediate loan on the Eurocurrency market of the foreign exchange to be earned. This can be sold at once for the spot price, the loan being repaid when the foreign importer pays his account.
8. Credit management is essential in export trade, and the services of an international credit reference agency should be employed to establish a credit rating for all customers. Trade indemnity insurance should also be considered.

3.11 Questions on Chapter 3

1. How are the prices of United Kingdom goods sold 'FOB London' calculated? Explain the elements entering into such prices.
2. 'The price for "delivered duty paid" goods must be higher than the "ex works" price.' Explain.
3. Distinguish between CFR and CIF contracts. Which price will be higher and why?
4. A telex message reads 'Please quote prices Mark 900 machine FOB, CFR and CIF terms. Also quote services mechanic erect and test *in situ*.' Discuss the ideas that enter into the various quotations.
5. 'Please quote FOB Incoterms 1980.' Explain the meaning of this request.
6. What is dumping? Why is it considered unfair? How can it be countered?
7. Why is it desirable to specify which currency a contract is to be expressed in? What advantages and disadvantages do 'currency baskets' have?
8. What are the basic ideas behind credit management? Refer in your answer to (*a*) the creditworthiness of the foreign buyer, (*b*) the special problems of dealing with companies, and (*c*) the establishment of credit ratings. Why is it particularly necessary in export trade?

Chapter 4
Payments in overseas trade I

4.1 Payments for exports

There is no point in exporting unless payment is actually secured for the goods or services supplied. It is sometimes difficult enough to get paid in the home trade. The problems are obviously increased when the customers are more remote, operate in a country where a different set of laws applies, speak a different language and pay in a foreign currency subject to exchange control and the vicissitudes of the foreign exchange market or where a state trading organisation insists on a 'barter' method of payment. Fortunately, not all our export activities are carried on in such unfavourable circumstances, but a great many of them are.

Over the years businessmen have developed systems of overseas trade which reduce the risks of non-payment to manageable proportions which can be covered by insurance in one way or another. These methods of payment range from 'open account' activities, in which the overseas customer is treated exactly like a respected and trustworthy home customer, to 'cash with order', in which nothing is done until payment has actually been received. We must become familiar with the procedures in each type of arrangement that is made.

In the list given below the possible arrangements for payment have been placed in the order of least risk. This does not mean that 'open account' actually entails more losses than the other methods, because, of course, you would not use that method if you could not completely trust the person at the other end. Perhaps it would be better to say that the methods below are listed in order of the trustworthiness of the distant customer, with the method advisable for a totally unknown customer placed first.

The arrangements are as follows:

(*a*) cash with order;
(*b*) export house transactions;
(*c*) documentary letters of credit;
(*d*) transactions using foreign bills of exchange
 (*i*) documents against payment,
 (*ii*) documents against acceptance;
(*e*) open account.

Each of these will be dealt with in turn in this chapter and Chapter 5. Since some of them require an understanding of bills of exchange and letters of credit, the use of these documents will also be explained.

Whatever method of payment is arranged, the parties have opposite attitudes to the arrangements. Ideally the exporter would like to be paid immediately. The importer would prefer to postpone payment until the very last moment, until the goods have actually arrived, or until they have arrived, been installed and been tested in operation. It depends very much whether it is a buyer's market or a seller's market as to which party will get the more favourable treatment. Generally speaking, the methods of payment that have become most widely accepted require the exporter to supply the goods up to a certain point, and if he supplies them in the way required, and up to specification, he will then obtain payment even if the customer has not yet received them.

4.2 Cash with order

If a customer wishes to purchase goods from a United Kingdom manufacturer, he may be prepared to pay 'cash with order', in which case the exporter has the benefit of immediate payment and proceeds to dispatch the goods or to manufacture them forthwith.

Clearly, this is a very favourable arrangement for the exporter. The importer is rarely willing to tie up his capital by parting with his money in advance in this way. Quite often, in countries where foreign exchange is controlled, the exchange control authorities will not sanction the payment until some tangible evidence that goods are on the way is made available. It is encountered, however, in a seller's market, where overseas firms are competing for the few goods becoming available.

The customer paying cash with order will transfer the funds to the exporter either by sending him a *banker's draft* or by means of a *bank transfer*. A banker's draft is simply a cheque made out by the banker instead of by the customer. If Mr Muhammad goes into his bank in Mombasa and asks them to draw him a banker's draft for £100 sterling, they will be happy to do so, provided there are no objections from the exchange control authorities. They will also send an interbank notification that the draft exists. Of course he will pay in ordinary Kenyan currency, and will have to pay a small charge for the trouble. He will then send the banker's draft to the exporter by airmail, along with his order. Note that this transfer is the importer's responsibility and that if the draft is stolen and misapplied he must carry the risk. Alternatively, he may simply ask the bank to arrange a credit transfer through the banking system, and charge him the cost in Kenyan shillings. The exporter in the United Kingdom is happy to receive the draft, or the credit transfer, which is certain to be honoured. He would be less happy to receive a personal cheque from Mr Muhammad and would not be prepared to supply the goods until the cheque had been cleared.

Once payment is received, the customer is, of course, entitled to receive the shipping documents as soon as they are available, for he has already paid for the goods. He will need the shipping documents before he can obtain the goods on arrival in Mombasa.

Payment of part of the price with the order is not uncommon, but is much less satisfactory than payment of the full amount when dealing with an unknown customer. It is therefore not advisable, but this type of part-payment may be a feature of very sophisticated large-scale capital projects, where the exporter would be unwilling to embark upon the project at all without some sort of financial inducement. In this case, 30 per cent of the total contract price might be paid as a deposit, the balance to follow in stages as the work proceeds.

In these days of high interest rates exporters of large capital items may find that 'part cash with order/balance on notification of readiness for shipment' terms increase their competitiveness. An initial 30 per cent deposit (*a*) ensures that the buyer will not default, (*b*) provides the seller with a large part of his working capital, thereby enabling him to reduce his actual selling price, and (*c*) brings home to the buyer just how expensive the usual long-term credit is.

4.3 Export house transactions

When export orders are handled by export houses, the foreign customer enters into the picture to only a very small extent. To all intents and purposes the export house is the customer and will pay the price in the home currency, although often the true principal in the bargain made is the foreign customer. It is difficult to be precise here, as the arrangements that are made vary. Let us first consider the term 'export house'.

4.3.1 *What is an export house?*

Export houses are firms specialising in the export of United Kingdom goods and are of two types, *merchant houses* and *confirming houses*. An export house operating as a merchant house – a merchant being one who actually buys goods and becomes their temporary owner – sells goods on its own account to the overseas customer. Thus, an export merchant buys like an ordinary home customer, and sells the goods overseas to customers who have no direct dealings with the United Kingdom manufacturer.

The other type of export house is the confirming house, which is often referred to as an 'indent house'. An indent is a requisition for goods, and may be either 'open' or 'closed'. A foreign customer who requires a particular class of goods indents for them to an export house, effectively asking the export house to act as its agent in the purchase of goods of the required type. If it is quite clear who manufactures the article, the manufacturer will be specified and the indent will be said to be 'closed'. Thus, an indent for Wilkinson Sword razor blades is a closed indent and must be passed through to that supplier, who will be approached and asked for a quotation. If the order had been for 'stainless steel razor blades' but no particular brand had been specified, the export house would have had discretion to shop around and obtain that class of goods from the supplier asking the most favourable price. This would be an 'open' indent. Notice that the export house is acting as the agent of the customer. If it is acting as a confirming house, it adds its good name to the transaction. Thus an open or closed indent which, as a result of negotiations, becomes an order for a certain class of goods at a specific price will be confirmed by the confirming house as if it was an order from them.

4.3.2 *Payment by export houses*

The two cases described above are very similar, in that in both cases the export house is effectively the buyer. It will therefore be prepared to pay the agreed price in home currency as soon as it takes over the goods. When this happens depends upon the terms of sale. It could be an 'ex works' price, or FOR, FOB or even CIF. However, since the export house often does its own packing, consolidating, documentation, etc., it is quite likely to be an 'ex works' price.

Wherever the change takes place, the exporter will perform his duties in the approved manner up to that point. For all terms of sale up to FOB the exporter will deliver the goods at the appropriate place, and tender the invoice. The confirming house or export merchant will then honour the payment. For CIF terms the exporter will ship the goods and tender the invoice supported by the shipping documents, i.e. the bill of lading, the insurance policy and any other documents, such as pre-shipment inspection certificates, certificates of origin or consular invoices, that may be required. On delivery of these documents the export house will pay the agreed price.

4.4 Documentary letters of credit

When a customer is not known particularly well to an exporter, but the transaction is being conducted directly and not through an export house, the use of a documentary letter of credit is a satisfactory way of ensuring payment before control of the goods is surrendered. The usual way in which this is effected is by an *irrevocable letter of credit* which may be *confirmed* in certain cases. It is prudent for each party to take out status enquiries on the other party during the negotiations leading up to the contract, before the credit is opened.

A really detailed understanding of letters of credit is necessary for all those engaged in international trade. Definitive statements about them are to be found in Brochure 290 of the International Chamber of Commerce entitled *Uniform Customs and Practice for Documentary Credits*, which may be purchased from the ICC (Brochures Department), Centre Point, 103 New Oxford Street, London WC1A 1QB. No student should be without a personal copy of this brochure, but the text is reproduced for reference by courtesy of the ICC in Appendix A.

4.4.1 *Arranging the credit*

Letters of credit are used when the relationship between importer and exporter is one of less than complete confidence, either because business between them is irregular or because the national situation of the importer's country is disturbed. During the course of the negotiations leading up to a contract this method of payment may be specified, and if the importer agrees he will approach his bank and ask them to set up the credit. The importer will specify the safeguards he wishes to be included in the letter of credit. Provided that exchange control permission is forthcoming if required, the bank will proceed to draw up the letter of credit, addressed to the exporter, and send it to its correspondent bank in the United Kingdom. They may request the UK bank to confirm the credit, which gives absolute security to the exporter, but whether this is in fact done depends to some extent on the bargaining strengths of the parties. An exporter selling a unique product in strong demand may be able to insist upon it. An exporter selling a product in a competitive market may have to accept an unconfirmed credit. Some of the developing countries, whose foreign exchange transactions are subject to severe control, refuse to allow confirmation since the UK bank naturally expects to charge for this service and it means a loss of foreign exchange to the developing country. The national bank of such countries, which is usually handling the transaction for one of its nationalised industries or state trading corporations, would probably justly claim that it is absolutely reliable anyway.

Credits may be revocable or irrevocable. The latter is to be preferred from the exporter's point of view, for it can be revoked only with the consent of all parties. A revocable credit may be revoked either by the importer or by the issuing bank if it becomes aware that its customer, the importer, is likely to default on the credit he has applied for.

4.4.2 *Parties concerned with a documentary credit*

The following are concerned with a letter of credit in the export trade.

(*a*) *The applicant*, who is the buyer of the goods, the foreign importer.
(*b*) *The issuing bank*, in the foreign country, issuing the credit on behalf of the importer.
(*c*) *The advising bank*, the correspondent bank in the country of the seller.
(*d*) *The confirming bank*, which is usually the same as the advising bank, but might be another bank in the seller's country. It adds its confirmation to the credit, to give the exporter absolute confidence in the transaction envisaged.
(*e*) *The beneficiary*, who is the seller or exporter of the goods.

4.4.3 *Nature of a documentary credit*

A documentary credit is an undertaking by a bank at the request of its customer, an importer, to pay an exporter or accept the exporter's term (usance) bill of exchange in respect of goods consigned to the importer when satisfactory documents including evidence of shipment and all other documents required under the terms of the credit are produced at a named place within a specified period. Clearly if this undertaking was given, and then five minutes later the bank withdrew its undertaking, i.e. revoked the credit, the exporter would not be very pleased, so the usual practice is to make the credit 'irrevocable'. A revocable credit is no real security at all, but it may be used where a customer of undoubted creditworthiness wishes to let an exporter know what funds are now available. If the credit is irrevocable it means that the customer has no power to cancel or amend the credit once it has been established, without the beneficiary's consent. So long as the exporter complies with the terms of the letter of credit in *every* particular to the satisfaction of the bank, then he will be paid out of the funds available. A documentary letter of credit is a contract between the parties to it, which is quite separate from the sale of goods which is connected with it and causes it to be made out. This contract is fulfilled by the presentation of documents in good order, evidencing that the goods have been shipped. Banks are not concerned with the goods themselves, for bankers do not want to be involved with the actual movement of the goods (though they may reserve the right to sell them in certain circumstances). The diagram in Figure 4.1 illustrates the typical sequence of activities for an unconfirmed credit. Note that if the credit had been an irrevocable *confirmed* credit, the UK bank would have released the payment at stage 7 in Figure 4.1, when an acceptable set of documents conforming with the requirements of the letter of credit was produced by the exporter.

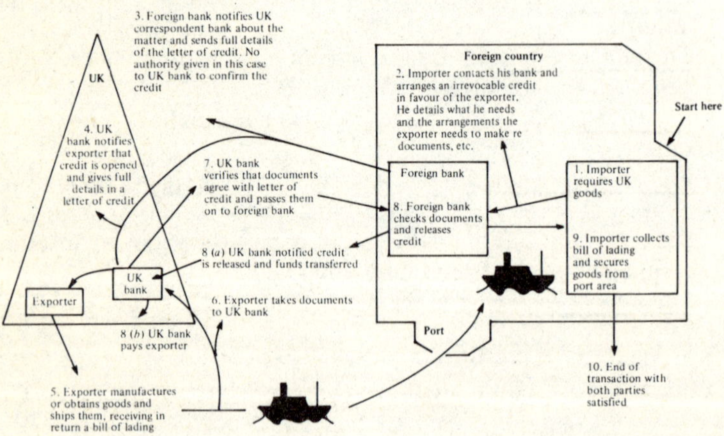

Figure 4.1 The sequence of events when an irrevocable unconfirmed documentary credit is used in international trade.

In the case of irrevocable credits, the issuing bank will often call for order bills of lading blank endorsed under which the consignee becomes a 'notify party' and therefore has access to the goods only through the issuing bank. This is essential as a safeguard in the case of countries where local law permits a named consignee access to the goods without the production of the relevant bill of lading.

4.4.4 *Confirmed and unconfirmed credits*

An unconfirmed credit becomes a confirmed credit when the name of a bank from the exporter's country is added to the undertaking already given by the foreign bank concerned. With international banks of undoubted reputation there is little need to confirm, but where there is any sign of political instability in the foreign country the confirmation of the undertaking by a home bank is desirable, but it does have to be paid for. It means that the exporter is put in funds as soon as he produces documents conforming with the letter of credit. With an unconfirmed credit the UK (or home) banking house receives and checks the documents. It then passes them on to the foreign bank, which will release the payment.

The letter of credit in Figure 4.2 should now be studied very carefully. It is typical of many letters of credit issued today, although the names are, of course, fictitious. For those not familiar with South American history, Garibaldi was an Italian soldier who played an important part in the liberation of some South American countries, and the name Garibaldia implies a South American country.

The student should notice the following points as he reads through the document in Figure 4.2.

(*a*) That the Excel Bank Ltd of London has had a credit opened with them by the Popular Bank of Garibaldia in favour of Goodbooks Ltd on behalf of the Commercial Partnership (Consorcio) Ltd of Garibaldia (the importer).

(*b*) That the amount of the credit is £2,000, it is valid until 3 September and the credit is a confirmed irrevocable credit.

(*c*) That the goods involved are described in Spanish after the word 'covering'. Part shipment is prohibited.

(*d*) That in order to receive payment the exporter must comply with the letter of credit, which requires him to produce the following documents in Spanish:

   (*i*) A full set of shipped bills of lading, marked 'Freight paid', and showing the amount paid. (A set might be three originals and twelve non-negotiable copies.)

Excel Bank Limited

Registered in England
(No. 00000)
Registered Office:
Lombard Street
London EC2P 2BX

Overseas Branch
PO Box 181760
70 St Mary Axe
London EC3P 3BN

Telephone 01-000 0000
Telex 000000 Telegrams Excelbank
London EC3
Extension 3259

Goodbooks Ltd
Camside
Cambridge

Date 8 August 19 . .

Advice of BANCO POPULAR DEL GARIBALDIA, INCAPAZ BRANCH, GARIBALDIA
Irrevovable credit which bears the confirmation of Excel Bank Limited

26 days

Dear Sirs,
We inform you that the above-named bank have opened with us their irrevocable credit in your favour on account of Consorcio Commercial de Garibaldia SA to the extent of £2,000.00 (two thousand pounds) valid at this office until 3 September 19 . . on or before which date your drafts on us at sight may be paid if accompanied by the under-mentioned documents evidencing current shipment from Liverpool to Yupanqui, Garibaldia, of the goods described below:

Part shipments prohibited. All documents to be in Spanish.

FULL SET OF SHIPPED BILLS OF LADING issued in favour of Banco Popular del Garibaldia, Incapaz, marked 'freight paid' showing the amount of freight paid.

CONSULAR INVOICE in 3 copies.

PACKING LIST in 3 copies.

COPY OF YOUR ADVICE sent to Consorcio Commercial del Garibaldia SA, advising details of shipment for insurance purposes.

COMMERCIAL INVOICE in 9 copies, showing the FOB value and freight charges separately.

COVERING: 2,800 piezas cajitas con envoltura de metal de 1 litro Nod. 16QH Partida Arancel: 98.15.01.00 – 96 piezas botellas de vidrio de 1 litro Nod. 14QF. Partida Arancel: 70.12.00.00.
C & F YUPANQUI, GARIBALDIA

We are informed that insurance will be covered by the buyers with Popular y Porvenir Cia. de Yupanqui.

Shipment must be effected in Garibaldian vessels or vessels of foreign companies who have a contract with Cia. Garibaldia de Vapores.

All drafts drawn under this Credit must contain the clause: 'Drawn under D/C No. 17.777,777'.

We are requested to advise you of the terms of the Credit which is irrevocable on the part of our principals, and also bears our confirmation. Subject to Uniform Customs and Practice for Documentary Credits (1974 Revision), International Chamber of Commerce Publication No. 290.

Figure 4.2 A letter of credit.

(*ii*) Three copies of a consular invoice.
(*iii*) Three copies of a packing list.
(*iv*) A copy of a letter sent by the exporter to the importer advising him to insure the cargo.
(*v*) Nine copies of a commercial invoice showing the FOB values and the freight charge (as this is on CFR terms).

(*e*) The insurance is being done by a Garibaldian insurer.
(*f*) The goods have to be carried in a Garibaldian ship, or one which has made arrangements with Garibaldia's State Steamship Line.
(*g*) It is made quite clear that the credit is confirmed, and the bank is authorised to pay the draft at sight. Payment is therefore absolutely certain, provided the documents are in strict conformity with the credit.
(*h*) Finally, the reader must note that the exporter will be bound by all the terms in the letter of credit, and if he has any objections or points to clarify he must do so at once. For example, if the letter of credit does not agree with the terms of his contract with the customer for the matter in hand, so that, for instance, he cannot manufacture the goods in time to meet the date of shipment, he must raise the matter at once. In Figure 4.2 the date of shipment is any time before 3 September, since documents presented by that date have to provide evidence of current shipment.

4.5 Checklists for letters of credit

A checklist is essential at all stages in the 'letter of credit' process, for serious responsibilities can fall upon those who fail to observe the terms of a letter of credit or negligently accept documents that are ineffective for some reason. The goods may be held up, or refused or even sequestrated in certain circumstances. For these reasons the greatest care is necessary.

The wide variety of arrangements possible makes it difficult to devise a perfect set of checklists, but those provided below are reasonably comprehensive. In each of the checklists that follow, put yourself in the position of the person or firm concerned and read the checklists from that viewpoint.

4.5.1 *Checklist for the exporter during the preliminary negotiations*

Although the exporter is not involved with a documentary credit until advised of its existence by the advising (correspondent) bank, the letter of credit comes into existence only because, in the pre-contractual stage, the exporter insists upon it. It is therefore essential for export staff on the sales side (as distinct from those trying to collect payment) to be knowledgeable about letters of credit and fully briefed about the exporting firm's usual practice in this respect. For this reason it is useful to have a checklist for the salesman before the contract is actually arranged.

(*a*) Is he aware of the distinction between an irrevocable and a revocable credit, and the fact that if a confirmed credit is wanted it must be irrevocable (since no bank would confirm a credit – and undertake an obligation to the beneficiary – if the credit could be revoked by the foreign issuing bank or the foreign importer)?

(*b*) Does he know the policy on letters of credit and whether he must insist on a confirmed credit?

(*c*) Should the credit be made available by payment, acceptance or negotiation? The ways in which the credit may be made available to the exporter are as follows:

  (*i*) by payment against documents;

  (*ii*) by payment against documents accompanied by a sight bill of exchange (a draft) drawn on a named paying bank (usually the issuing bank, but possibly the advising bank);

  (*iii*) as an acceptance on a term (i.e. usance) bill of exchange drawn on the issuing bank payable at a certain date (e.g. 30, 60 or 90 days after date or after sight) presented for acceptance with the documents within the time-limit set by the credit;

  (*iv*) by negotiation. A negotiation credit is one where the issuing bank undertakes to pay the drawer, endorsers or other bona fide holders of a bill associated with the credit. Thus, an exporter may take the documents and his bill drawn on the foreign importer or the issuing bank to any bank prepared to negotiate it for him. The exporter will be paid the full value; the negotiating bank becomes a holder in due course entitled to be paid by the issuing bank provided the documents comply with the credit and were negotiated within the time-limit. Since the issuing bank is reputable, there is usually no need for recourse against the exporter.

(*d*) Where is the credit to be payable (in the United Kingdom, or elsewhere)?

(*e*) What currency is to be used and what are the implications of this on the contract being arranged?

(*f*) He must be aware of how important exactness is in the detailed arrangements, particularly:

(*i*) The correct name of the beneficiary company, its spelling and the address.

(*ii*) The exact details of the goods – names, quantities, reference numbers, prices and total value – although these should be kept as simple as possible.

(*iii*) The total value of the letter of credit.

(*iv*) The date of expiry, which must be extensive enough to permit manufacture, testing, packing and shipping.

(*v*) The arrival of the credit, which must be early enough to permit the activities mentioned in (*iv*) above to be carried out.

(*vi*) The method of notification (airmail, telex, etc.) must be laid down, and ICC 290 should be specified to control the behaviour of the parties to the credit.

(*vii*) The mode of transport influences the requirements of the letter of credit. For example, multi-modal transport gives a degree of freedom to the combined transport operation (CTO) to select routes, ports of departure, etc. Transshipment should be allowed if the transit is multi-modal. Ports of departure and arrival become places of taking-in-charge and delivery and ports of shipment and destination should not be stated. The salesman must also know whether part-shipments are allowed and, if so, whether this means that part of the credit can be released.

If air transport is envisaged, the letter of credit should state whether a forwarder's or house air way bill is acceptable.

(*viii*) The types of document required, and the numbers, and the particular requirements of the country concerned.

(*g*) Must the cargo be shipped on deck? If it must, whether because of awkward size, hazardous nature, etc., it must be permitted 'on deck' shipment in the letter of credit and the insurance policy.

(*h*) Some countries require inspection, test running and so on before packing. In these cases it is as well to establish exact names, addresses and qualifications of those required to sign the certificate. Also, if they are to pack and load after testing, this should be specified, as should the name of the party who is to pay the costs, which may need to be built into the contract price.

(*i*) It is important to establish personal contact between the two firms, and to note the names, telephone numbers and extensions of each contact so that problems can be sorted out simply and quickly, avoiding delays which may render the credit out of date before payment can be obtained by the submission of documents.

4.5.2 *Checklist for the importer (applicant for the credit) when applying*

(*a*) Has a status report on the supplier been taken out to verify his ability to supply goods of the type and quality required?

(*b*) Has the contract been thoroughly vetted to ensure that the exact requirements as to the quantity, specification, delivery date, terms of sale, terms of payment, etc., are known?

(*c*) Before applying for the credit to be established, has the question of finance to honour the credit been carefully considered and are funds available or budgeted for in a proper manner?

(*d*) In completing the application form, have we ensured that every instruction necessary for efficient conduct of the bank's undertakings has been covered? In particular:

(*i*) Is the credit to be revocable or irrevocable?

(*ii*) Is it to be confirmed by a bank in the seller's country?

(*iii*) How is the credit to be advised? Airmail?

(*iv*) What is the amount and currency of the credit, in words and figures?

(*v*) For how long is it to be valid and how and where is it to be paid?

The credit may be made available to the exporter in the following ways:

(*i*) by payment against documents;

(*ii*) by payment against documents accompanied by a sight bill of exchange (a draft) drawn on a named paying bank (usually the issuing bank, but possibly the advising bank);

(*iii*) as an acceptance on a term (i.e. usance) bill of exchange drawn on the issuing bank payable at a certain date (e.g. 30, 60 or 90 days after date or after sight) presented for acceptance with the documents within the time-limit set by the credit;

(*iv*) by negotiation. This has been explained in section 4.5.1 (*c*) (*iv*). The issuing bank undertakes to honour the credit not only to the beneficiary but to any other party in possession of a valid bill of exchange associated with the credit, holding as a holder in due course for value and who negotiated the documents within the time-limit of the credit. The exporter is financed (i.e. paid in full) at the negotiating bank, which can be any bank prepared to act. The place of validity of the credit is not specified in the credit, and the negotiating banker's premises become the place of validity. Although the issuing bank is liable to honour the bill, in practice it will usually be honoured on the issuing bank's behalf by the advising bank.

(*e*) He must know what documents are required. Two are obligatory. They are the invoice *expressed in exactly the same terms as the letter of credit* and a document of movement *as proof of shipment, air freighting or multi-modal transport.* Other documents may include:

(*i*) Proof of origin or value, or both.
(*ii*) Proof of insurance (or, if applicant is insuring, a letter or telex to notify applicant of shipment details in good time for cover to be arranged).
(*iii*) Proof of pre-shipment inspection, weighing, analysis, etc.
(*iv*) Proof of packing, and/or conformity with indent.
(*v*) Proof of health, freedom from pests, etc.
(*vi*) Consular invoices.
(*vii*) A copy of the export licence if applicable.

(*f*) What are the details of the goods required, including price per unit if applicable?

(*g*) Are export licences necessary and if so is the supplier aware that he is responsible for them?

(*h*) Are import licences necessary and if so are they in hand at this (i.e. the importer's) end? The licence number should be quoted in the letter of credit.

(*i*) What are the terms of trade, and are Incoterms 1980 to be specified?

(*j*) Are part-shipments allowed and is trans-shipment permitted? It is inadvisable to restrict the latter if multi-modal operations are being used, since the carrier is holding himself responsible for any losses, and restricting his choice of ships and routeing may lead to delay. The routeing description should be general, i.e. the United Kingdom port should not be specified.

(*k*) If the exporter is to insure, is it clear what level and value of cover is required? Must it be a Lloyd's policy?

(*l*) Are any other dates apart from the date of expiry of the credit important? For example, is there to be a time-limit on the date of shipment or on the gap between shipment and presentation of documents? If the latter gap is more than 21 days, the documents are considered stale.

(*m*) Are there any restrictions on the flag of the ship chosen?

4.5.3 *Checklist for the issuing bank when granting the credit*

(*a*) Is the applicant known to us, and creditworthy to the extent of the amount required? Has he an established line of credit? Does this request exceed it and, if so, what steps should we take?

(*b*) If the credit is revocable, we can revoke it ourselves if at any time we fear that the applicant has ceased to be worthy, but if it is irrevocable we shall be bound by it and consequently must be sure of the applicant's reliability.

(*c*) Has the applicant signed our (i.e. the bank's) usual indemnity form, and a certificate of pledge giving us rights over the document of title, the goods themselves and an active right to sell the goods if he defaults?

(*d*) Any queries re ambiguities, inconsistencies or omissions must be raised (see the checklist for importers in section 4.5.2).

(*e*) Draw up a letter of credit for the correspondent bank in the exporter's country (the advising bank), ensuring absolute accuracy in all respects, particularly names, addresses, details of goods, prices and values, list of documents, details of amount, validity, time, place and method of payment of credit; all dates and details re part-shipments, trans-shipment, etc., should be checked.

(*f*) Is the consignment insured in a proper manner? Since the consignment represents part of our security for the credit, on which we, as issuing bank, may be liable, damage in transit may leave us with worthless goods in the event of the customer's default. It is therefore important, especially with FOB or CFR contracts, that our importer insures the goods in time after the exporter has notified the details of shipment as required by Incoterms. On CIF terms the exporter must produce a valid insurance document when he presents the documents after shipment.

(*g*) Is the import licence in order? If the goods are refused entry because no import licence has been issued, the security for these operations is unable to enter the jurisdiction of our courts.

If all the points listed are in good order we should notify the credit by the method prescribed in the application. This means we will telex, airmail or facsimile copy detailed instructions to our correspondent bank in the exporter's country asking them to notify the exporter that the credit is available.

4.5.4 *Checklist for the advising bank (and also the confirming bank)*

When the credit arrives we must check it carefully to see that all necessary items appear to have been raised (see the checklist for importers in section 4.5.2). If confirmation is being requested, we are undertaking a commitment to the beneficiary which we will be obliged to honour. We must therefore look to the status of the issuing bank and the stability of the country concerned. If we are unsure about this, we must require the transfer of funds from the issuing bank. These funds will be held in a suspense account until the credit is honoured.

(*a*) We must advise the exporter of the existence of the credit, referring particularly to the following points:
  (*i*) At whose request are you advising him? (This means naming the issuing bank.)
  (*ii*) The exact terms of the credit as laid down by the applicant (see section 4.5.2).
  (*iii*) Whether it is revocable or irrevocable, and if it is irrevocable whether we are to confirm it or not. If not, we have no engagement personally to provide funds for the beneficiary.

(*b*) We must also deal with any changes notified by the issuing bank as a result of protests by the exporter, and advise the exporter of them so that he is reassured and can proceed with the order.

4.5.5 *Checklist for the exporter on receipt of the credit*

(*a*) The exporter must check the letter of credit when it arrives from the advising bank to see whether it conforms with the original agreement with the foreign customer as to the following points:
  (*i*) Revocable or irrevocable.
  (*ii*) Confirmed or unconfirmed.
  (*iii*) Are the names and addresses of the parties as expected, and are they spelt correctly?
  (*iv*) Does the shipping date specified give sufficient time to manufacture or obtain the goods, pack and ship them?
  (*v*) Is it a sight or term credit? If the latter, what is the period of usance?
  (*vi*) Does the expiry date give enough time to prepare and present the documents?
  (*vii*) Is the amount sufficient to cover the original quotation and any variable items specified in it? Is the currency correct and the place of validity?
  (*viii*) Is the description of the goods correct?

(*ix*) Is partial shipment permitted if necessary?
(*x*) Is the port of final discharge as agreed?
(*xi*) A list of documents and a note of which language is to be used. Bill of lading? Air way bill? Parcel post receipt? Export licence? Is a copy required? Invoice? Consular invoice? Packing list? Packing certificate? Certificate of origin? Certificate of value? Certificate of inspection? Certificate of quality? Veterinary certificate? Phytosanitary certificate? Certificate of weight? Certificate of age? Insurance policy or certificate with appropriate clauses? Certificate of analysis? If import licence is required, has the number been quoted to show that it has been issued?
(*xii*) If 'on deck' shipment is needed, does the letter of credit authorise it?
(*xiii*) If a vessel is being chartered, does the letter of credit specify that a charter party bill of lading is acceptable?
(*xiv*) Are the terms of the sales contract in accordance with the original Incoterms specified in the contract?
(*xv*) Are the transport documents correct for the mode of transport envisaged?
(*xvi*) Does the letter of credit call for an insurance policy or an insurance certificate? Does it call for notification to the foreign insurer who will arrange cover?
(*xvii*) Are all the licence and documentation requirements of a country met (see Croner's *Reference Book for Exporters*)?
(*xviii*) See also the checklist in section 4.5.1 for further details.

(*b*) Raise any queries direct with customer and urge him to send immediately authorised amendments via his issuing bank, for onward transmission to the exporter.

(*c*) (*i*) Proceed to manufacture or obtain, assemble and pack the goods.
(*ii*) Process documents in accordance with the letter of credit.
(*iii*) Ship goods according to the letter of credit.
(*iv*) Obtain a bill of lading or other document proving dispatch of goods.

(*d*) (*i*) Present documents to the advising bank in accordance with the letter of credit, including sight draft for payment or term draft for acceptance or negotiation.
(*ii*) If credit is not a confirmed credit it may be necessary to wait until payment is remitted or 'accepted' term bill arrives from abroad before funds can be obtained.

(*iii*) Acknowledge conclusion of contract to importer and solicit further business.

4.6 Difficulties on presentation of documents

The whole idea of a letter of credit is that a sum of money (the credit) is made available to an exporter, provided he fulfils the requirements of the letter of credit as to the provision of certain documents evidencing shipment or other forwarding movement of goods ordered by the importer. The vital thing is exact compliance with the instructions in the letter of credit, hence the necessity to correct it at once if there is anything wrong with it on arrival or it is not in accordance with the arrangements originally made by the salesman. Even when there is a correct letter of credit, a number of difficulties may arise on presentation of the documents. A list of the chief possible problems and discrepancies is given below, but first let us stress that routine slips in such items as names, addresses, details of the goods and so on can be reduced by the use of *aligned documentation*, in particular the forms prepared and approved by the Simplification of International Trade Procedures Board (SITPRO). A word about these is desirable at this point.

The SITPRO Board is an official organisation in the United Kingdom charged with the responsibility of simplifying international trade procedures, which it does by representing the United Kingdom in international discussions about overseas trade activities. Aligned documentation is the major part of this simplification and it seeks to persuade everyone interested in overseas trade to adopt a standard pattern of document, so that the same information appears in the same place on every form. There are perhaps 20 or 25 pieces of information which appear on almost every form. For example, the name of the exporter will be found on every document concerned with an export, whether it is an invoice, a bill of lading or an air way bill. Clearly, it will be easy to find the exporter's name if it is always printed in the same place on every form. The whole area of an A4 sheet of paper has been divided by a United Nations Committee into a number of fields, each of which is labelled to take a specific piece of information; for example, the consignee's name appears in field 2. Every document designed by anyone in the world should use field 2 for this piece of information if it is needed. If a particular document does not need the consignee's name, then field 2 becomes a 'free disposal' area for that form and can be used for any purpose. Thus, a warning might be printed in field 2 if a particular difficulty is met on that form, or it might be specified there that it is essential to complete six copies of the document.

Having decided on the use of every field on the paper, it is possible to prepare a *master document* from which all other documents can be run off. The master document is masked to exclude any details that are not required on a particular form, so that each form finally contains only the information it requires and nothing else. Therefore, once the master document has been carefully checked, every form will bear the correct spelling and exact details, and copying errors cannot cause discrepancies between the documents which might cause a bank to reject the documents and refuse payment.

A SITPRO Master Document is reproduced in Figure 4.3. The address of the SITPRO Board is given in Chapter 9.

Checklist of possible problems and discrepancies

1. Letter of credit expired It is essential to present the documents within the expiry date of the letter of credit, but since the bank itself has onerous responsibilities it must have a reasonable length of time to examine all papers before the letter of credit expires and therefore they should be presented without delay as soon as they become available. Progress of all outstanding documents should be chased daily, and the use of an *export data folder*, such as the one produced by Formecon, helps to ensure that daily checks are made to follow up documents which are pending. (Formecon's address is given in Chapter 9.)

2. Late shipment If shipment is required by a particular date in the letter of credit and the deadline is not met, the banks will not release the credit. The exporter will then have the problem of getting the importer to extend the letter of credit, which means added cost at least, and possibly other problems.

3. Late presentation If the letter of credit specifies that documents must be tendered within a time-limit after shipment, failure to do so means that the documents will be rejected. Since the goods are already on their way, this leads to numerous problems. The whole point of asking for a letter of credit – security of payment – has been lost by inefficiency in the documentation section of the export department.

4. Absence of documents Documents must be produced as required and in the necessary numbers.

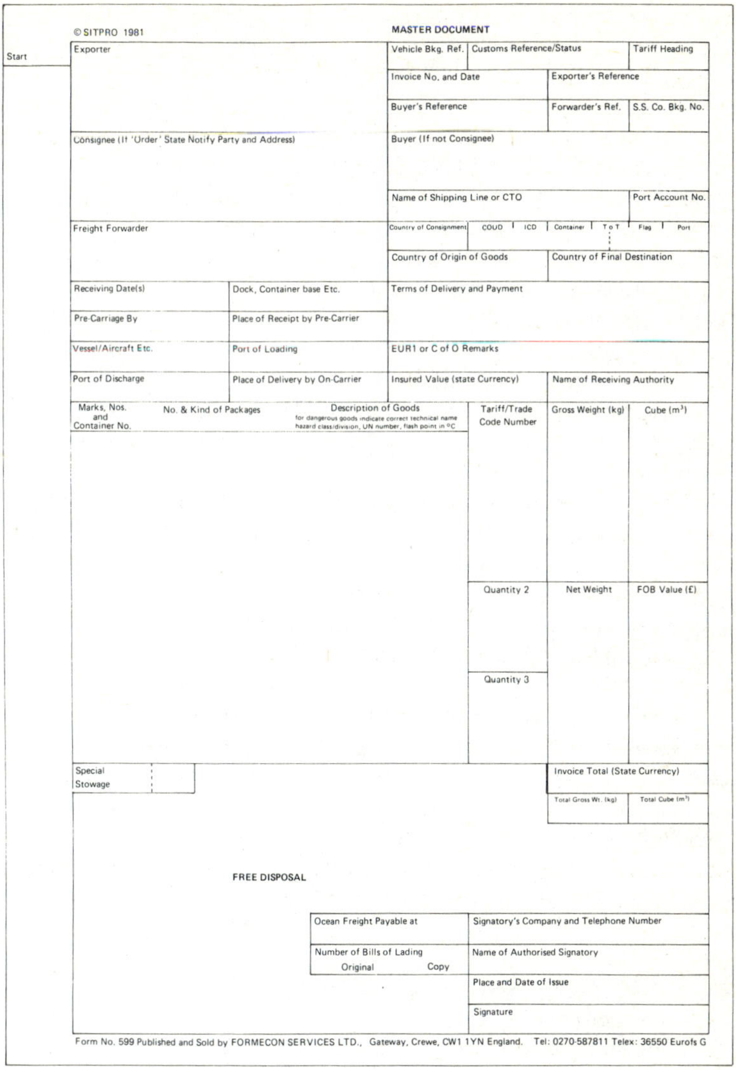

©SITPRO 1981

MASTER DOCUMENT

Start

Exporter

Vehicle Bkg. Ref. | Customs Reference/Status | Tariff Heading

Invoice No. and Date | Exporter's Reference

Buyer's Reference | Forwarder's Ref. | S.S. Co. Bkg. No.

Consignee (If 'Order' State Notify Party and Address)

Buyer (If not Consignee)

Name of Shipping Line or CTO | Port Account No.

Freight Forwarder

Country of Consignment | COUD | ICD | Container | T o T | Flag | Port

Country of Origin of Goods | Country of Final Destination

Receiving Date(s) | Dock, Container base Etc. | Terms of Delivery and Payment

Pre-Carriage By | Place of Receipt by Pre-Carrier

Vessel/Aircraft Etc. | Port of Loading | EUR1 or C of O Remarks

Port of Discharge | Place of Delivery by On-Carrier | Insured Value (state Currency) | Name of Receiving Authority

Marks, Nos. and Container No. | No. & Kind of Packages | Description of Goods for dangerous goods indicate correct technical name hazard class/division, UN number, flash point in °C | Tariff/Trade Code Number | Gross Weight (kg) | Cube (m³)

Quantity 2 | Net Weight | FOB Value (£)

Quantity 3

Special Stowage

Invoice Total (State Currency)

Total Gross Wt. (kg) | Total Cube (m³)

FREE DISPOSAL

Ocean Freight Payable at | Signatory's Company and Telephone Number

Number of Bills of Lading Original Copy | Name of Authorised Signatory

Place and Date of Issue

Signature

Form No. 599 Published and Sold by FORMECON SERVICES LTD., Gateway, Crewe, CW1 1YN England. Tel: 0270-587811 Telex: 36550 Eurofs G

Figure 4.3 A SITPRO Master Document

5. *Defective documents* Sometimes documents are provided, but they are found to be defective in some way. This means that they do not comply exactly with the requirements stipulated. The following are examples.

(*a*) A dirty bill of lading may be provided when a clean bill is called for. A dirty bill of lading is one claused with some remark, such as 'appears contents broken on loading' or 'packing cases stained and wet'.

(*b*) A 'received for shipment' bill of lading may be provided when the credit calls for a 'shipped on board' bill of lading. Order bills of lading should be blank endorsed.

(*c*) The vessel, flag or port of departure or arrival may not be in agreement with the letter of credit.

(*d*) The goods may have been shipped on deck when this is not permitted by the credit.

(*e*) The wrong insurance document may have been provided, or inadequate cover may have been arranged, regarding the amount, type, extent or currency of cover. In the case of CIF contracts, or cost and insurance contracts, the document must be endorsed to give the importer the benefit of the cover obtained.

(*f*) There may be errors on the bill of exchange, such as the wrong party drawn on, the wrong amount, inadequate dating, incorrect endorsement.

(*g*) Signatures may be absent, or inadequate signatures for the country concerned, such as facsimile signatures, may have been given when original signatures are required.

6. *Inconsistent documents* Documents must be not only correct themselves but also consistent with one another, particularly as to names, addresses, spelling, description of the goods, weights, volumes and values, including total value, marks and numbers.

Definitive checklists about documentary credits may be obtained from SITPRO. Details are given in Chapter 9.

4.7 Final stages in the letter of credit procedure

4.7.1 *The confirming bank*

(*a*) On receipt of documents, check carefully to ensure that they conform with the credit, especially with respect to such items as those included in the list of common discrepancies given above.

(*b*) If the credit is a confirmed credit, pay the sight draft or 'accept' term bill if this is being used.

(*c*) Discount the term bill at the exporter's expense (unless the buyer has agreed otherwise) if he desires it.

(*d*) Transmit documents to issuing bank by airmail.

4.7.2 *The issuing bank*

(*a*) When the documents arrive from the correspondent bank, check to see that they conform exactly with the letter of credit.

(*b*) If the credit was unconfirmed, pay sight draft by mail transfer or telegraphic transfer, or accept usance bill of exchange (or arrange acceptance by importer if drawn on him).

(*c*) If the credit was confirmed, arrange to reimburse the confirming bank by crediting its account, or by crediting a foreign currency account, or by any other method.

(*d*) Call in the importer and release the documents against settlement of the credit arranged on his behalf.

4.7.3 *The importer*

(*a*) When called into the bank, take delivery of the documents against release of payment.

(*b*) Collect the goods from the port and undertake control of them to their destination.

(*c*) If they are damaged or deficient in any way, take appropriate claims action. (Ensure that claims and legal actions are commenced within known time-limits according to the mode of transport used so as to safeguard the insurer's position on subrogation. Failure to do this may lead to a claim for negligence.)

4.8 Other types of credit

In the sophisticated affairs of businessmen a variety of arrangements can be made which facilitate business activities. As far as letters of credit are concerned, besides the irrevocable credits described above, which may be confirmed or unconfirmed, the following arrangements may be made.

4.8.1 *Transferable credits*

A transferable credit arises where a middleman exporter is operating between a supplier and a foreign importer, rather like a confirming house but without wishing to carry the financial responsibility for making payment for the goods. The middleman agrees to supply the foreign importer with goods at a certain price, intending to obtain the goods from a supplier at a lower price. The difference between the two prices will be his eventual profit. The original credit authorises the correspondent bank to accept instructions from the prime beneficiary – the middleman – to transfer some of the benefit to one or more secondary beneficiaries. The original letter of credit, made out with the middleman as prime beneficiary, is transferred partly into a credit for the supplier at the lower price. The supplier is now the second beneficiary. He manufactures or obtains the goods, packs them, etc., and presents his documents to the bank for payment. The bank, having checked the documents, now honours the credit for the supplier. It then calls on the exporter to modify the documents by substituting his own invoice for the supplier's invoice. The middleman's invoice is, of course, at the full export price and renders the documents in conformity with the original letter of credit issued by the foreign bank. This credit is honoured – minus the portion already paid to the supplier – giving the middleman his profit. The documents are then sent by airmail to the foreign bank. The United Kingdom end of these transactions is illustrated Figure 4.4.

Where a transferable credit is to be transferred to more than one secondary beneficiary, they will both have to ship goods before they

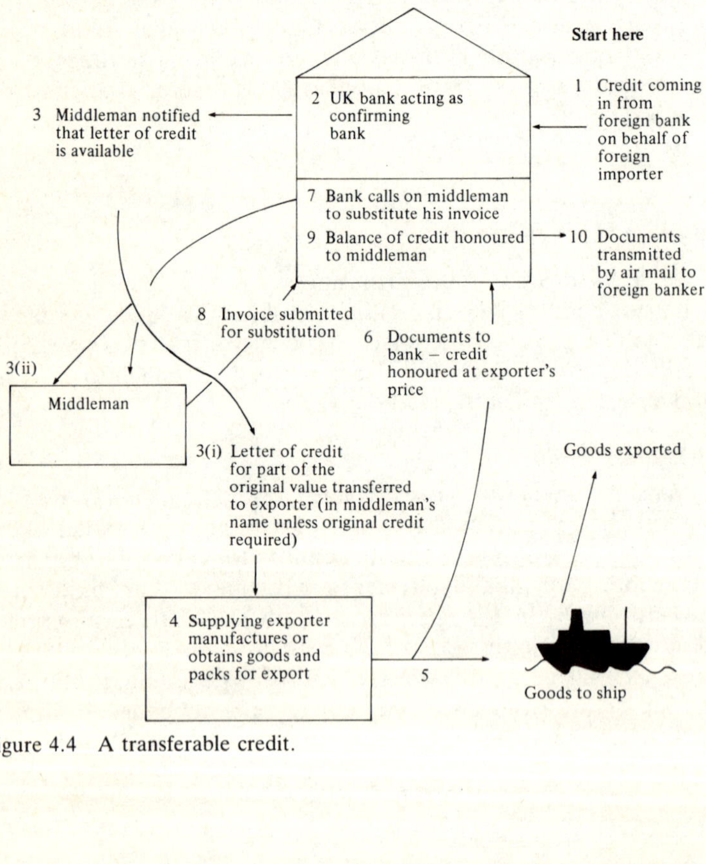

Figure 4.4 A transferable credit.

can produce documents entitling them to be paid. This means that the original credit must be of the type that permits part-shipment. If part-shipment is not allowed there can be only one secondary beneficiary.

Article 46 of the 1974 revision of the *Uniform Customs and Practice for Documentary Credits* gives a full explanation of transferable credits, and is well worth close study (see Appendix A).

4.8.2 *Back-to-back (also called countervailing) credits*

Back-to-back credits are credits where a second credit to a second beneficiary is made out on the strength of an already existing credit in favour of a first beneficiary. Imagine that A in Australia arranges a credit for B in the United Kingdom so that B can supply him with hardboard from J in Sweden. It may be more convenient for B to arrange a credit for J in Sweden on the strength of the credit already in existence from Australia. This saves B becoming personally committed and enables J to be paid from the original credit. The pattern of activities is illustrated in Figure 4.5. Like the transferable credit described above, the back-to-back credit provides the fund

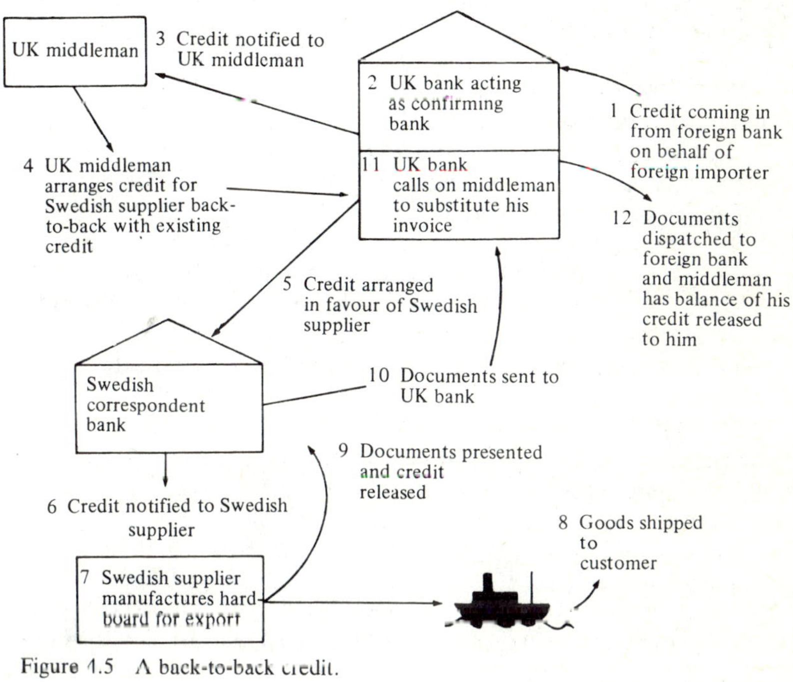

Figure 4.5 A back-to-back credit.

for the credit of the secondary beneficiary from the temporarily immobilised fund for the credit of the first beneficiary.

4.8.3 *Revolving credits*

These are used when a regular series of shipments takes place and the parties wish the series to proceed without interruption. A credit is opened for a known sum in a known period, say £10,000 per month. As shipments take place against it, the credit is eroded, but a further replenishment of the credit will be available as the new month begins. The credit usually is non-cumulative, that is any unused balance from the previous month is not carried forward, but a cumulative credit would allow the new £10,000 to be added to any previous unused balance. With improved communication there is less need than formerly for this type of automatic renewal of a credit.

4.8.4 *'Red clause' credits and anticipatory credits*

Red clauses (so called because they were written in red ink on the credit) are used in the wool trade and certain other trades where exporters have to collect a cargo together by buying at auctions or direct from farmers or planters. The exporter may obtain part of the credit as and when required before shipment. On final tender of the shipping documents the balance of the credit is released.

4.8.5 *Personal credits*

Personal letters of credit enable those named in them to draw money without delay from a bank or agent up to a limit specified in the letter. A signature will be required which must agree with the specimen signature previously furnished to the agent or bank. If the letter of credit is acceptable in a large number of branches or agencies, the person to whom the letter is issued will carry on him a 'letter of indication', which contains his signature and indicates to the agent that he is the person authorised to draw money. A credit card, now commonly in use, is a form of letter of indication.

4.8.6 *Negotiation credits*

Negotiation credits (see section 4.5.1 (*c*)) are credits (often issued by merchant banks which do not have a branch banking system) where the issuing bank makes an undertaking along the following lines: 'We hereby engage with the drawer, endorsers and bona fide holders that each draft drawn under, and in compliance with, the terms of the said credit, and accompanied by the above-specified documents, will be duly honoured if *negotiated* on or before the expiration date.' The exporter presents his documents and a bill of exchange drawn on the foreign importer or the issuing bank to his local branch of a commercial bank. This branch becomes the place of validity of the credit, and the bill is paid in full. The negotiating bank then holds the bill as a holder in due course for value, and is entitled to collect the amount due on its own account, with interest, from the issuing bank. The advising bank in the exporter's country is not concerned once the exporter has been advised, but in practice it may honour the bill on the issuing bank's behalf.

A negotiation credit therefore differs from an ordinary credit in that the issuing bank engages to pay other people (endorsers and holders in due course) rather than just the beneficiary under the credit. Ordinary credits may still be negotiated by the advising bank: the bank buys the bill from its customer (the exporter) but interest and charges will be for the exporter's account and recourse in the event of dishonour will be against the exporter. Recourse rarely arises under a negotiation credit since the issuing bank is worthy.

4.9 Payments for imports

In the description of overseas payments given in this chapter constant reference has been made to the foreign importer and his position with regard to payment. In paying for goods purchased from overseas the importer follows the same procedure as any foreign importer buying British goods. The terms on which he will pay must be agreed with his supplier beforehand and he will then follow the pattern of conduct already described. Thus, in letters of credit he will set up the credit, stipulating the documents to be provided, as given in the checklists in section 4.5.

4.10 Summary of Chapter 4

1. The most common methods of payment include cash with order, export house transactions paid on delivery to the export house, documentary letters of credit, payments using bills of exchange and open account transactions.
2. Cash with order requires the importer to pay at once before any work on fulfilling the order begins. It is the least favourable method for the importer and can be insisted upon only in a seller's market.
3. Export houses buy either for their own account or as confirming agents for the foreign importer, against orders or indents from abroad. They then pay in the home currency either against goods, or, if the goods have been forwarded, against the documents of title which represent the goods.

4. The irrevocable letter of credit is a means of reducing payment risks in overseas trade. The importer sets up a credit for the exporter from which the exporter can be paid, provided he delivers to the bank holding the credit a full set of documents evidencing shipment. The documents required are specified in the letter of credit. If payment is confirmed, it will be paid in the United Kingdom by the confirming bank. If it is not confirmed, the advising bank will transmit the documents to the issuing bank, which will then release the credit. There are many types of credit, including sight credits, acceptance credits, transfer credits, back-to-back credits and revolving credits.
5. It is essential to work through a checklist for letters of credit to ensure that all the important aspects have been noted and complied with. A comprehensive list of the most likely discrepancies is available from the Simplification of International Trade Procedures Board at the address given in Chapter 9.

4.11 Questions on Chapter 4

1. What are the common methods of payment in international trade? Arrange them in the best order from the point of view of the exporter, naming first the most certain method of payment, and so on.
2. What is meant by 'cash with order'? Compare the importer's and exporter's views of 'cash with order' transactions.
3. Distinguish between an 'export merchant' and a 'confirming house'. How is payment made for goods exported through these two types of export house?
4. What is an irrevocable confirmed letter of credit? What safeguards does it give to (*a*) the importer, and (*b*) the exporter?
5. What is a back-to-back credit? Use as an example an order from an Australian importer to a British exporter of Swedish motor cars.
6. Write at least six lines on *three* of the following:
   (*a*) revocable credits,
   (*b*) confirmed credits,
   (*c*) trans-shipment,
   (*d*) part-shipments.
7. How would an importer establish a letter of credit in favour of an overseas supplier? What would he need to specify in the letter to reassure his foreign supplier? What would he need to specify to ensure all was well from his own point of view?

Chapter 5
Payments in overseas trade II

5.1 Collections: transactions using foreign bills of exchange

The two ways of obtaining payment from the customer by using bills of exchange are known as documents against payment and documents against acceptance. Before we can understand these arrangements it is necessary to understand exactly what a bill of exchange is, and why it is such a useful commercial document. Let us therefore turn our attention to these points.

5.1.1 *What is a bill of exchange?*

The answer to this question is given in Section 3 of the Bills of Exchange Act 1882. It seems at first glance to be a very long and involved definition. In fact it is an almost perfect definition, as good as any group of Parliamentary draftsmen has drafted. The reader is strongly recommended to learn it by heart. It takes about five minutes to learn perfectly and once you get it into your head you will never forget it. It says:

> A Bill of Exchange is an unconditional order in writing, addressed by one person to another, signed by the person giving it, requiring the person to whom it is addressed to pay on demand, or at a fixed or determinable future time, a sum certain in money to, or to the order of, a specified person or to bearer.

Do learn it by heart. What it means exactly can be followed best by looking at a typical bill of exchange. For simplicity's sake the example shown in Figure 5.1 and considered here is an inland bill. A foreign bill is discussed later.

With reference to Figure 5.1 we can see the following.

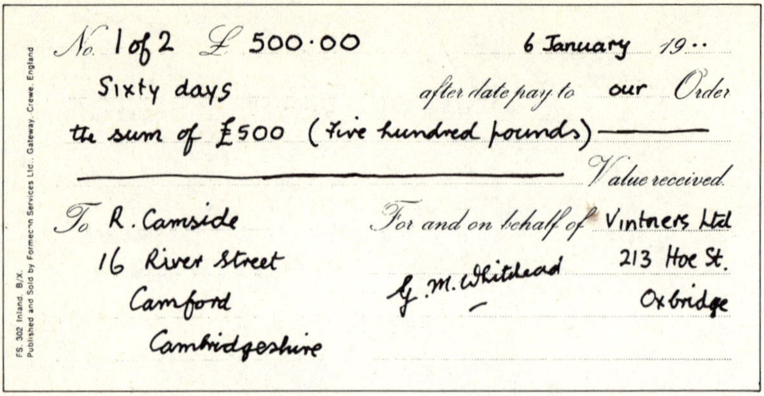

No. 1 of 2 £ 500·00 6 January 19··

Sixty days after date pay to our Order

the sum of £500 (five hundred pounds)

Value received.

To R. Camside For and on behalf of Vintners Ltd

16 River Street 213 Hoe St.

Camford G. M. Whitehead Oxbridge

Cambridgeshire

FS. 302 Inland. B/X.
Published and Sold by Formecon Services Ltd., Gateway, Crewe, England

Figure 5.1 An inland bill of exchange.

(*i*) 'A bill of exchange is an order in writing'. . . We can see that it is, and it tells R. Camside to pay £500.

(*ii*) 'A bill of exchange is an *unconditional* order in writing'. . . It does not say 'provided the good ship *Peerless* reaches Liverpool' or anything like that. It just says 'pay' – whatever happens. There is no doubt that R. Camside knows what he has to do. It is unconditional.

(*iii*) . . .'addressed by one person to another'. . . We can see that this written order is addressed to R. Camside from Vintners Ltd.

(*iv*) . . .'signed by the person giving it'. . . We can see that G. M. Whitehead has signed it on behalf of Vintners Ltd, who are giving the order to R. Camside.

(*v*) . . .'requiring the person to whom it is addressed'. . . This is, of course, Mr Camside.

(*vi*) . . .'to pay on demand, or at some fixed or determinable future time'. . . In this case it is not on demand (a sight bill) but at a fixed or determinable future time, because it says 'sixty days after date'. That is 60 days after 6 January 19. . . We will assume that 19. . was not a leap year so that 60 days after 6 January is 7 March. The bill is therefore payable on that date. It used to be the custom that three days' grace were added – to make up for the dreadful conditions of the roads in the early days when bills of exchange were first invented. This has now been discontinued, but still applies in some countries where the idea was copied from the United Kingdom. In such countries the bill would become payable on 10 March.

(*vii*) . . .'a sum certain in money'. . . Mind you don't read this incorrectly. It doesn't say 'a certain sum'; it says 'a sum certain'. Thus, if I made out an order telling someone to pay me the value of a flock of sheep, when they were actually sold in Oxbridge market the order would not be a bill of exchange. A bill of exchange has to be 'a sum certain' – for example, £500 – not the value of a flock of sheep.

(*viii*) . . .'to, or to the order of, a specified person or to bearer'. In this case it says 'pay to our order', which means that on the due date we will let you know who to pay the money to.

(*ix*) The number on the top of the bill is used to indicate which one of a set of bills this is. When bills are issued in sets like this they are sent off by successive posts, and when one of them is honoured, the others become void. Thus, they are all equally valid, but the first to be presented is the one that is accepted.

If the reader has worked carefully through this explanation he will now see what a splendid definition of a bill of exchange it is. A bill of exchange is not just any written order; it has to be an unconditional order in writing, etc., etc.

5.1.2 *The parties to a bill of exchange*

There may be many parties to a bill of exchange, but the chief ones are (*a*) the drawer, (*b*) the drawee, who usually becomes the acceptor, and (*c*) the payee.

The drawer is the person who draws (writes out) the bill. In Figure 5.1 it is Vintners Ltd. Anyone who writes his name on a bill of exchange is bound to honour the bill, and therefore the drawer – who must sign the bill when he writes it out – is immediately liable upon it by signing his name in this way. Of course, he does not want to honour it; he expects the drawee to honour it.

The drawee is the person drawn upon and in Figure 5.1 it is R. Camside. R. Camside may not even know that the bill is being drawn, and it is possible to draw a bill on a fictitious character, like Robinson Crusoe. If I draw a bill on Robinson Crusoe, it is not very likely that he is going to turn up and honour it on the due date. But it can still be a good bill, because my name is on it as drawer, and so long as the drawer is honest, the bill is sound. Such fictitious drawees are rare, however, and normally the drawee knows about the bill, and is expecting to honour it. He will usually show this intention by 'accepting' the bill. This means he takes the bill and either writes 'Accepted' and his own name on it, or just signs it. So the drawee has now become the acceptor, and the bill has two good names on it.

The third possible party is the payee. The payee is the person named who is to be paid the money on the due date. Frequently it is the same person as the drawer, the bill reading 'pay me' or perhaps 'pay us'. In Figure 5.1 it says 'pay to our order', which means 'pay the person we tell you to pay on the due date'. An 'order' bill can be passed on, or negotiated, by a process called endorsing. To endorse is to write on the back. Thus, to endorse a bill I would write 'Pay Tom Jones' and sign it G. M. Whitehead. If you just sign it, the bill is said to be 'endorsed in blank' and becomes a 'bearer' bill, and can be passed freely from hand to hand. This is not really satisfactory, as the holders do not need to add their names to the bill. Remember, everyone who writes his name on a bill is bound to honour it, so the more names it has the better. It is unlikely that they are all going to be made bankrupt for the sake of £500, or whatever the value of the bill happens to be.

We have now mentioned another really important point about bills of exchange. You must honour them. If you do not, you cannot expect to remain in business, for you have broken a solemn promise to pay. The person who dishonours a bill will be dealt with in a formal way which results in bankruptcy.

If the acceptor dishonours the bill, then the next person must honour it. The drawer must pay, for he is the one who was silly enough to do business with the acceptor who has dishonoured. The drawer cannot expect other people to honour the bill when he has received value for it and it is his customer who has dishonoured the bill.

5.1.3 *The usefulness of bills of exchange*

The next thing is to decide exactly why bills of exchange are so useful. The explanation, presented in diagrammatic form in Figure 5.2, is that they oil the wheels of business and commerce by extending credit through the money market to reliable firms who would otherwise have to operate at a less than optimum level.

With reference to Figure 5.2 we can see the following.

(*i*) If one businessman (in our illustration a retailer) wishes to obtain goods for re-sale without paying for them immediately, he may be allowed by the supplier to do so and in return he agrees to accept a bill of exchange.

(*ii*) Suppose that the supplier manufactures the goods for £2,250 and agrees to sell them at £3,000 to A. Retailer. He supplies the goods, and draws a bill on A. Retailer for £3,000. Retailer accepts the bill, signing his name on it and thus agreeing to honour the bill on the due date.

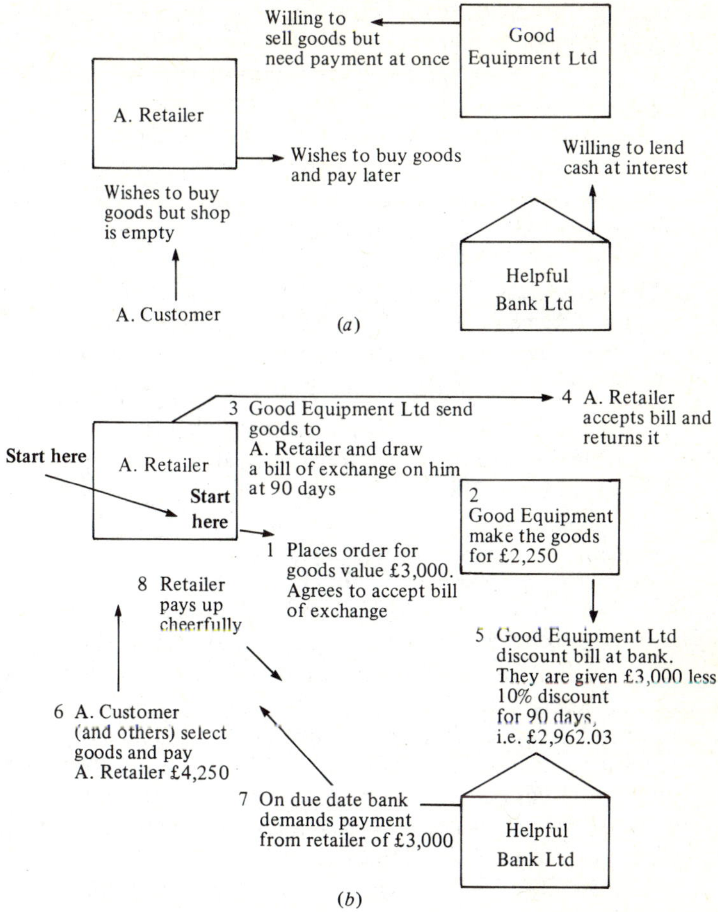

Figure 5.2 (*a*) The problem. (*b*) Solving problems with a bill of exchange.

(*iii*) Retailer can now proceed to sell the goods, adding a profit margin. In this case we are supposing that the goods sell for £4,250.

(*iv*) Meanwhile, the manufacturer has discounted his bill of exchange with the bank at 10 per cent. This means that he sells it to the bank less 90 days' interest at 10 per cent per annum. The bank therefore gives him £2,926.03 for the bill. The manufacturer endorses the bill over to the banker and the bank will add it to its portfolio of short-term investments.

(*v*) On the due date the bank asks Retailer to honour the bill, and he pays the £3,000

(*vi*) Consider the positions of each of the parties to this series of transactions:
- The manufacturer has engaged in a profitable transaction at a profit of £676.03.
- The retailer has engaged in a profitable transaction at a profit of £1,250.
- The bank has loaned £2,926.03 for 90 days and earned interest of £73.97, which works out at $10\frac{1}{4}$ per cent per annum.
- The customers of A. Retailer have been able to buy goods which otherwise would not have been available and are experiencing the satisfactions of the consumer society.

It can be seen from this illustration and the above notes that the chief advantage of an inland bill of exchange is that it promotes the level of business activity, encouraging deals to take place by providing a freely negotiable document acceptable to everyone and relying absolutely on the need to honour it on the due date.

With foreign bills, this advantage still applies. The exporter who can afford to give his customer credit on the bill – in other words use a term (or usance) bill – and knows that his customer is reliable, can keep the wheels of his industry turning in this way. The other advantage of the foreign bill of exchange is that it enables the exporter to keep control of his goods (through the use of his bankers) until the time of payment (documents against payment) or of acceptance (documents against acceptance). Alternatively, if he has sufficient confidence in his customer, so that withholding the documents is not necessary, he may simply use the bill of exchange as a means of prodding the importer into payment, by sending a 'clean' bill for collection. A 'clean' bill is one unencumbered by documents.

We must now consider these three methods of securing payments for exports.

5.2 Documents against payment (D/P)

As has already been explained, the letter of credit is one way of ensuring that payment is received for the goods we export. It is, however, a very detailed process, requiring the foreign importer to make very careful arrangements, which we, as exporters, must then observe faithfully. This can be tedious, especially between businessmen who have been engaged in a succession of transactions, possibly over many years, and have considerable confidence in one another. A more simple arrangement is to use the bill of exchange as a means of securing payment either at once (documents against payment) or after giving the exporter a limited amount of credit (documents against acceptance).

The use of documents against payment is most suitable in the following circumstances.

(*a*) Where the exporter wishes to ensure that he does in fact receive payment at once for the goods supplied. This may be because he has some doubts about the reliability of his customer or the political and economic stability of the country with which he is dealing. Alternatively, he may be selling on a seller's market, in which case there is no reason at all why he should not demand payment at once, for if this particular customer cannot pay, someone else will be delighted to buy the goods.

(*b*) Where the exporter himself wishes to obtain finance (a loan from the bank) in the interval between shipment and payment. A bank holding documents of title to which a sight bill is attached has a very good security and will often therefore sanction a loan.

This system of securing payment is also of benefit to the importer, in that it is an improvement on cash with order or a letter of credit. For instance, his capital is not tied up until he actually takes delivery of the documents, as it would be with 'cash with order', and the arrangements he has made with his own bank do not commence until a 'collecting banker' approaches him for payment. At this time the importer may pay the collecting banker, but if he has no funds available he may approach his own bank for assistance, which may take the form of a 'merchandise advance' (sometimes called a reimbursement draft if obtained from a merchant bank). The goods represented by the documents are pledged to the bank, which thus holds the title to the goods. When the importer is ready to handle the goods, the documents are released against a 'trust receipt', under which the importer becomes an agent of the bank for the disposal of the goods. Should anything go wrong in the sales transaction, the bank can sue in its own right, as principal. If all is well, the proceeds of the sale cover the advance with interest and the importer receives any balance there is.

5.3 Documents against acceptance (D/A)

Here, a term bill or usance bill is used instead of a sight bill. This is exactly like the inland bill illustrated in Figure 5.1 and serves the same purpose. It gives the importer time to pay the bill, and the opportunity to sell the goods and obtain the money needed, with a profit for himself besides. It is most useful in the following circumstances.

(*a*) Where the market is a buyer's market, so that unless terms of credit are offered the customer will turn elsewhere. This is very often the situation today, and competitiveness on credit terms is a particular feature of competition from countries such as Japan, and the controlled economy countries.

(*b*) Where the integrity of a customer is without doubt and the costs of waiting for payment can by agreement be charged to the customer, or alternatively have been allowed for in the quotation, where they form only a small part of the profit margin.

In these circumstances the exporter has obtained business which he might not otherwise have obtained, and has at least the satisfaction of obtaining an accepted bill of exchange which he can discount on the money market. Since a customer dishonours a bill at his peril, this is a reasonably secure method of payment. The consequences of dishonour are much more immediate and effective than the consequences of delaying payment or defaulting on an ordinary contractual debt, as for example with open-account transactions.

A difficulty can arise if the documents are presented by the collecting bank as soon as they receive them since this may interfere with the credit arrangements made between the exporter and his customer. Usually these allow long enough for the goods to be sold before payment, or long enough for them to be turned into manufactured goods and then sold. Since the agreed days start to run from the date of acceptance, the customer is losing time if the goods have not yet arrived. In these circumstances it is usual to ask the bank to wait until the goods arrive before presentation for acceptance.

5.4 Clean collections

Where an exporter requests the collection of money from an importer without any documents being attached to the bill of exchange or promissory note, it is called a 'clean' collection. The documents evidencing shipment or air forwarding have been sent direct to the importer abroad, who is entitled to collect the goods on arrival. The exporter sends the bill or note to his bank, requesting collection. His bank then becomes the *remitting bank* and sends the bill to its correspondent bank in the importer's country. This bank is called the *collecting bank*, and if it then presents the bill for collection it becomes the *presenting bank*. Provided funds are forthcoming, the payment will be relayed back to the remitting bank, which will credit the account of the exporter with the relevant sum, less any charges incurred that were payable by the exporter. A collecting bank may use another bank as the presenting bank.

5.5 Collection procedure

When bills of exchange are to be passed to a bank for collection, the process is controlled by the 1978 *Uniform Rules for Collections*. These rules are published by the International Chamber of Commerce and are reproduced by courtesy of the ICC in Appendix B. They should be carefully studied by the reader, since they give a definitive view of what should happen provided the rules do not contravene the particular laws of a given state. The rules relate to two types of remittances – 'clean' remittances and 'documentary' remittances. For clean remittances (described above) the bank has only the simple duty of collection to perform. With 'documentary' bills there are other duties involved, such as handing over the documents against payment or acceptance.

To ensure that clear instructions are given, the rules say that commercial paper sent for collection must be handed over to the collecting bank with a covering letter, which is usually drawn up as a form with a specified layout. This letter from the remitting bank is called a remittance letter. They in turn have been instructed by the exporter on a form called a documentary collection form. Typical collection forms are reproduced in Figures 5.3 and 5.4 (see pages 100–3) by courtesy of the SITPRO Board.

Looking at Figures 5.3 and 5.4, the reader will note the various boxes which the exporter must use to give his instructions. When the collection form is completed the exporter must give careful instructions about anything likely to cause difficulty, for example whether the goods are to be landed and warehoused in case of non-payment or non-acceptance. If the space labelled 'in case of need refer to' is used to name a local representative who may be consulted in case of trouble, it is best to define the powers of this representative. Most of these powers will be understood from the references made to the matters above.

One point not explained earlier is the question of 'protest'. This is the legal consequence of dishonouring a bill, whether by non-payment or by non-acceptance. It involves the use of an official

FOREIGN BILL AND/OR DOCUMENTS FOR COLLECTION

AUTHORISED BY THE BRITISH BANKERS' ASSOCIATION

Drawer/Exporter	Drawer's/Exporter's Reference(s) (to be quoted by Bank in all correspondence)
Consignee	Drawee (If not Consignee)
To (Bank)	For Bank use only

FORWARD DOCUMENTS ENUMERATED BELOW BY AIRMAIL. FOLLOW SPECIAL INSTRUCTIONS AND THOSE MARKED X

Bill of Exchange	Comm'l. Invoice	Cert'd./Cons. Inv.	Cert. of Origin	Ins'ce Pol./Cert.	Bill of Lading	Parcel Post Rec'pt.	Air Waybill
Combined Transport Doc.	Other Documents and whereabouts of any missing Original Bill of Lading						

RELEASE DOCUMENTS ON	ACCEPTANCE	PAYMENT	If unaccepted →	Protest	Do Not Protest
If documents are not taken up on arrival of goods	Warehouse Goods	Do Not Warehouse	and advise reason by	Cable	Airmail
	Insure Against Fire	Do Not Insure	If unpaid →	Protest	Do Not Protest
Collect ALL Charges			and advise reason by	Cable	Airmail

Collect Correspondent's Charges ONLY		Advise acceptance and due date by	Cable	Airmail
Return Accepted Bill by Airmail		Remit Proceeds by	Cable	Airmail
In case of need refer to			For Guidance	Accept their Instructions

SPECIAL INSTRUCTIONS: 1. Represent on arrival of goods if not honoured on first presentation.

Date of Bill of Exchange	Bill of Exchange Value/Amount of Collection
Tenor of Bill of Exchange	
Bill of Exchange Claused:—	Please collect the above mentioned Bill and/or Documents subject to the Uniform Rules for Collections (1978 Revision), International Chamber of Commerce,Publication No. 322. I/We agree that you shall not be liable for any loss, damage, or delay however caused which is not directly due to the negligence of your own officers or servants.
	Date and Signature

447

Figure 5.3 The SITPRO foreign bill and/or documents for collection form.

INCORPORATING BILL OF EXCHANGE

ADDITIONAL COPY FOREIGN BILL AND/OR DOCUMENTS FOR COLLECTION

Drawer/Exporter	Drawer's/Exporter's Reference(s) (to be quoted by Bank in all correspondence)
Consignee	Drawee (If not Consignee)
To (Bank)	For Bank use only

FORWARD DOCUMENTS ENUMERATED BELOW BY AIRMAIL. FOLLOW SPECIAL INSTRUCTIONS AND THOSE MARKED X

Bill of Exchange	Comm'l. Invoice	Cert'd./Cons. Inv.	Cert. of Origin	Ins'ce Pol./Cert.	Bill of Lading	Parcel Post Rec'pt.	Air Waybill

Combined Transport Doc.	Other Documents and whereabouts of any missing Original Bill of Lading

RELEASE DOCUMENTS ON	ACCEPTANCE	PAYMENT	If unaccepted →	Protest	Do Not Protest
If documents are not taken up on arrival of goods	Warehouse Goods	Do Not Warehouse	and advise reason by	Cable	Airmail
	Insure Against Fire	Do Not Insure	If unpaid →	Protest	Do Not Protest
Collect ALL Charges			and advise reason by	Cable	Airmail

THIS FORM SHOULD ONLY BE USED IN CONJUNCTION WITH THE BRITISH BANKERS' ASSOCIATION APPROVED FORM "FOREIGN BILL AND/OR DOCUMENTS FOR COLLECTION"
(SEE "Systematic Export Documentation", SITPRO 1976)

Collect Correspondent's Charges ONLY		Advise acceptance and due date by	Cable	Airmail
Return Accepted Bill by Airmail		Remit Proceeds by	Cable	Airmail
In case of need refer to			For Guidance	Accept their Instructions

SPECIAL INSTRUCTIONS: 1. Represent on arrival of goods if not honoured on first presentation.

SITPRO OVERLAYS 1981

447/490
Tear

Date of Bill of Exchange

BILL of EXCHANGE for

At

Pay against this sole of exchange to our order the sum of:

DRAWEE

FOR VALUE RECEIVED

Signature

Figure 5.4 A collection form incorporating a bill of exchange.

called a public notary, who writes out a written statement that the bill was not honoured by the drawee, or the acceptor, whichever is the case. The wording of the bill is copied out into the official 'protest'. This protest is then evidence of dishonour, and may be used to commence legal proceedings. Protest is explained more fully in a companion volume entitled *Elements of Export Law*, also in the 'Elements of Overseas Trade Series'. Although strictly speaking a remitting bank does not have any legal duty to examine documents to ensure that they are in good order (unlike the situation where a letter of credit is in use), the preservation of customer goodwill makes it desirable to check the documents. The following is a list of difficulties that may arise.

(*a*) Documents listed in the collection order may not have been presented, and there is an obligation under the rules for banks to check that these have, in fact, arrived.

(*b*) Where documents are issued in sets, it is important that no member of the set is missing, since any missing document may have already reached the foreign importer or some third party who could use it to claim the goods. The instructions to the bank include details of what to do in the event of non-payment or non-acceptance, and if some third party claims rights to the goods it may be impossible to follow the exporter's instructions.

(*c*) Correctly drawn bills of exchange and correctly endorsed shipping documents are important since any defects will become apparent as soon as we try to execute the documents concerned.

(*d*) The terms of trade used may impose certain requirements. Thus, CIF demands that an endorsed insurance document is presented with the set of documents to cover at least the full invoice price. CFR and CIF require that the document of movement be marked 'Freight paid'.

(*e*) As with letters of credit, the requirements of the importing country regarding import licences, consular invoices, packaging materials, etc., must be met.

The following important points from the 1978 *Uniform Rules for Collections* should be borne in mind.

(*a*) In using another bank to make a collection the remitting bank is only the agent of the principal requiring funds to be collected and the collection is made for the account of, and at the expense of, that principal. The principal is liable to indemnify the bank for any expenses and responsibilities arising from foreign laws or usages.

(*b*) The banks adopt into their contracts with the principal exemptions from many liabilities, such as those arising from acts of God, civil commotions, loss of documents and so on.
(*c*) If instructions are not clear about the release of documents, the banks will only release documents against payment.
(*d*) If the payment is in local currency, the banks will release the documents only if the money paid is available for immediate disposal as instructed in the collection order. This also applies if the currency of payment is a foreign currency other than the importer's currency.
(*e*) In advising the fate of any collection, the bank reserves the right to use electronic means at the expense of the principal if this seems desirable in the circumstances.

It is highly desirable that students work through the actual wording of the *Uniform Rules for Collections*, given in Appendix B. Copies of the brochure (No. 322) are available from the International Chamber of Commerce at the address given in Chapter 9.

5.5.1 *Negotiation*

Sometimes the bank agrees to negotiate the bill for the exporter. This is a special use of the word 'negotiate' which normally means 'pass on to another party'. In this case it means that the bill is purchased from the exporter by the bank, who thus becomes the holder in due course of the bill. A 'holder in due course' is one who takes the bill in good faith for value, and who is consequently entitled to claim payment on his own behalf, and to sue on the bill if it is dishonoured. Therefore the form for lodging bills which are to be negotiated does not contain any boxes (as in Figure 5.3) about 'If unaccepted/unpaid protest', or 'If unaccepted/unpaid do not protest'. Instead, the bank reserves the right to use its own discretion to protest the bill, for it has become the true 'holder in due course' for value.

Besides its rights as a holder in due course, and its rights as the possessor of the actual documents of title which represent ownership of the goods, the bank usually insists also upon other safeguards. In the form for lodging foreign bills for negotiation there is a clause which expressly permits the bank to 'realise the goods in case of need'. The word 'realise' means dispose of them at the best price obtainable. There is also a clause which makes it quite clear that the bank has the right to 'recourse', meaning that it has the right to claim back the money advanced to the exporter when the bill was discounted. It would, of course, have that right in the normal way on any bill of exchange which was dishonoured. Finally, the bank may demand a letter of hypothecation.

5.5.2 *Letter of hypothecation*

The word 'hypothecation' is derived from a Greek word and means 'security over a thing belonging to a debtor'. When the bank negotiates the bill for the exporter there is a chance that he will eventually become the bank's debtor should the bill be dishonoured. However, taking from him a pledge that the property concerned may be sold to realise the money owed, or at least some contribution towards the money owed, the bank secures written evidence of its rights to sell the property. A *general* letter of hypothecation refers to any negotiations the bank may carry out for the exporter. A *specific* letter of hypothecation refers to a particular transaction only.

5.5.3 *Collection charges*

Inevitably there are collection charges such as stamp duty, postage and telex charges, administrative charges, exchange rate conversion charges and even interest charges for the days between payment of the money and its receipt in the United Kingdom. It is a matter of agreement, depending on the bargaining situation of the parties, as to who will pay such costs. The exporter should always attempt to get his customer to agree to bear these charges, but if this is impossible, he should include them in the price so that they are reasonably covered anyway.

5.5.4 *Exchange clauses*

'A bill of exchange is an unconditional order in writing', etc., etc., so that one would not expect to find conditions and clauses attached to a bill of exchange in the same way that they are to a bill of lading or other carrier's document. However, clauses referring to the rate of exchange to be used are sometimes encountered, since they form part of the process of determining the 'sum certain' which is to be paid on the bill. It might be argued that without an exchange clause any sum mentioned is to some extent uncertain. In these days of floating exchange rates no one can be quite sure what they will actually receive on the bill of exchange they make out, unless they specify it absolutely.

A bill expressed in sterling may be claused in one of the following ways.

(*a*) *Payable at the current rate of exchange for sight drafts on*

London, plus all bank charges. The current rate of exchange will be the rate prevailing on the day of payment and the drawee must also pay the bank charges. The drawer gets the face value of the bill, in sterling.

(*b*) *Payable at the collecting bank's selling rate for sight drafts on London*. The drawee pays the face value of the bill at the rate of exchange set by the collecting banker, and the drawer receives the face value of the bill less the collection charges.

(*c*) *Payable with interest at x per cent per annum from date hereof until the approximate date of arrival of the remittance in London*. This is the so-called 'Eastern clause', less commonly used today than in the past since money moves so quickly around the world that there need really be no delay. It has legal disadvantages in that it infringes the rule about a bill of exchange being for a 'sum certain': if the time the interest is to run has to be estimated, it cannot be certain, and might lead to the courts declaring the bill to be outside the Bills of Exchange Act 1882.

(*d*) *Exchange as per endorsement*. This clause is used in the negotiation of sterling bills. It leaves the bank – which has paid the exporter the full face value of the bill – to insert an exchange clause in such a way that it receives from the drawee in his own currency a sum sufficient to cover all its costs including interest on the advance it has made to the drawer. The drawee is bound to accept these charges, but since he is paying in his own currency it is the bank which is bearing the exchange risk. The bank covers itself by selling forward. Thus a sterling bill has been converted into its foreign currency equivalent plus charges, and this amount is written above the sterling amount.

Finally, it must be said that clauses should not be used unless the foreign customer has given at least tacit approval: clauses which are inappropriate to a particular country, or trade, or to which the customer has not agreed will only cause delay and annoyance to a valued customer. Where the customer has agreed to pay all charges, stamp duty, etc., a clause to this effect will ensure that the profit on the transaction is not reduced by such expenses.

5.6 Open-account transactions

Where perfect confidence exists between exporter and customer in stable economic conditions 'open account' transactions take place in which the customer is treated like any home-based creditworthy customer, dealing under the usual terms for that class of business.

Very often this means 'cash 30 days', in other words cash is payable within one month after the account has been rendered at the end of the month. The shipping documents are sent direct to the customer, who can claim them at once and proceed to market them. The exporter relies on his relationship with the importer to secure payment in due course, and on the stability of the country concerned with regard to international settlements. Note that the finance of this type of overseas trade usually rests on the normal arrangements prevailing in the home trade – the exporter has sufficient liquid reserves to offer the importer credit for the agreed period.

Settlement is made in due course. The importer may send a cheque to the exporter, which he will pass to his bank as a 'clean' collection. Alternatively, the importer may purchase a banker's draft, or arrange for his bank to transfer funds by airmail or telex to a correspondent bank in the exporter's country.

A second system of 'open account' which gives slightly better control of the customer is to deal on open account but draw a bill of exchange on the customer for each shipment. This means that the agreed period of credit is allowed by the 'usance' bill and there is no likelihood of the debtor dragging out payments and taking an extended period of credit. The threat that a bill will be protested if it is dishonoured on the due date is sufficient to ensure that payment will be forthcoming.

5.6.1 *Protest*

Section 51 (2) of the Bills of Exchange Act says that a foreign bill must be protested if it is dishonoured by non-acceptance or by non-payment. If it is not protested, the other parties whose names are on the bill, i.e. the drawer and any subsequent endorsers, are discharged from any responsibility on the bill. Since the holder of a bill of exchange will usually look to these parties for recourse, and call upon them to honour the bill, it is essential to preserve these rights by immediate protest of the bill. The protest also becomes firm evidence for the courts that the bill was presented and dishonoured for the reasons stated in the protest.

The protest is a deed, drawn up by a notary public evidencing the fact that he presented the bill for acceptance or payment, and it was dishonoured for the reasons given in the protest. The bill is copied out into the protest, which is signed by the notary. If the bill could not be presented because the drawee, or acceptor, could not be found, this fact must be recorded.

Section 48 of the Act requires notice of dishonour to be given to the drawer and any endorsers who may become liable on the bill. If notice of dishonour is not given, the parties concerned are discharged from liability. Notice may be given personally or in writing within a reasonable time.

5.6.2 *Trading with subsidiaries*

Open-account transactions may take place when a holding company trades with foreign subsidiaries and when there can clearly be no question of lack of confidence between the parties. Trading is frequently two-way, with the records kept on open account and the net indebtedness position only needing to be settled at the end of the open account period. Such trading can, of course, also take place between firms which are not part of a parent–subsidiary relationship, for example where manufacturers of similar products in different countries engage to market the others' products in their own countries.

5.7 Summary of Chapter 5

1. Payment for exports may be obtained with bills of exchange. The definition of a bill of exchange is very important and should be learned by heart. Because a bill of exchange is binding upon those who sign it and because the legal consequences of default are severe, a businessman is unlikely to dishonour his promise to pay.
2. Bills of exchange are collected under arrangements laid down in the International Chamber of Commerce's *Uniform Rules for Collections*. The usual methods are 'documents against payment' and 'documents against acceptance'. A foreign bill collection form is used to instruct the bank about the procedure it is to follow. These instructions are conveyed to the collecting banker abroad in a 'remittance letter' from the remitting banker.
3. Clean collections are collections unencumbered by documents. The exporter has sent the documents direct to the importer abroad, thus forfeiting his control of the goods, and merely requires the bank to collect the payment, possibly a foreign cheque, or payment of a sight bill of exchange.
4. With documents against payment transactions, the bank will instruct the collecting banker to release the documents to the foreign importer only against payment in full, in currency that is readily transferable to the exporter.
5. With documents against acceptance, the bank will instruct the collecting banker to release the documents against acceptance of

a usance bill of exchange. This gives the foreign importer a period of credit before the bill becomes payable.

6. Negotiation of a bill may be arranged so that the exporter is paid the full face value of the bill when it is presented with the documents. The bank then proceeds with the collection in its own name, as holder in due course, but it reserves a right of recourse against the exporter in the event of non-payment, and also takes a pledge from him entitling the bank to sell the goods in the event of non-payment.
7. Bills of exchange may be claused with 'exchange' clauses which help to decide the 'sum certain' for which they are valid.
8. When a foreign bill is dishonoured it must be protested, that is the dishonour is recorded in a legal document which acts as formal evidence in the courts. Notice of dishonour must be given to the drawer and any endorsers of the bill.
9. Open-account transactions permit the foreign customer to pay by banker's draft or credit transfer in the normal course of business activity, like any home debtor.

5.8 Questions of Chapter 5

1. Define a bill of exchange. Explain its popularity in international trade as a means of obtaining payment.
2. What is meant by the phrase 'documents against acceptance'? How would an exporter who exported goods D/A after drawing a 90-day bill obtain payment at the due date? Could he obtain the use of his money before the due date?
3. Write at least ten lines on three of the following:
   (*a*) bills of exchange,
   (*b*) protests,
   (*c*) documents against payment,
   (*d*) collection forms.
4. Why are exchange clauses used on bills of exchange? Explain how such a clause could destroy the fundamental character of the bill of exchange.
5. What are 'open account' transactions? How may the date of payment on open account be made more definite?
6. What is meant by 'cash with order' and 'open account dealing'? Compare these from the point of view of the exporter.

Chapter 6
Financing overseas trade

6.1 The problem of financing overseas trade

The term 'financing overseas trade' refers to the difficulties attending the conduct of overseas trade in the time interval between agreement on the contract and payment on completion. Every business faces this problem, in both home and overseas trade. The normal way to finance business activity is by the use of the capital provided by the owners of the business. In early times this meant the sole trader or the partners who had established the business. Today it usually means the shareholders who contribute the capital of the company, and the debenture holders who lend the company money for the conduct of its affairs. However, it is possible to borrow money for the conduct of business from other people than shareholders or debenture holders; for example, overdrafts and bank loans may be arranged. Whether it is wise to do this depends very much on the profitability of the proposed activity, bearing in mind that borrowed money has to be paid for and the lenders of finance cream off some of the profits leaving the owners to enjoy only the residue. Thus, if the business is very profitable, the interest on money borrowed to finance it will hardly be noticed; if the business is not very profitable, the interest will cream off nearly all the profit leaving the exporter with little for himself.

The time-lag between the commencement of the contract and payment for it varies with the type of contract. The usual short-term contract for the sale of goods is completed within six months – and often much sooner. Contracts settled in up to two years are regarded as short term. Medium-term trade is usually regarded as any time between two years and five years, while long-term contracts are those in excess of five years. Very long credit periods may sometimes be arranged for long-term capital projects, to keep United Kingdom credit policies in line with those of her major competitors.

Where goods are sold under an agreed method of payment such as an irrevocable letter of credit or using bills of exchange D/P or D/A, the payment date will arrive relatively quickly, and the period during which the exporter's operations must be financed is quite short. Such periods may conceivably be financed by the exporter himself using his own capital. Alternatively, he will be able to use the ordinary finance facilities available to any owner of a valid bill, negotiating it or discounting it to achieve the use of the funds at once (less interest for the agreed period). This facility is not available to those offering longer credit terms. Few firms can afford to finance long-term contracts out of their own capital and must accordingly seek assistance from some outside source.

Listing the means of financing overseas trade in some sort of logical order, and including methods of short-term finance that have already been mentioned, we have the following methods of raising capital:

(*a*) finance from the firm's own capital resources, if necessary by floating off a new issue of shares or debentures,
(*b*) finance by normal overdraft facilities or longer-term bank loans,
(*c*) finance by negotiation,
(*d*) finance from advances against collections,
(*e*) finance by acceptance credits,
(*f*) finance by ECGD short-term bank guarantee,
(*g*) non-recourse finance by an export finance house,
(*h*) finance by factoring,
(*i*) finance by invoice discounting,
(*j*) medium-term finance (two to five years) through banks and other institutions, and through ECGD 'lines of credit',
(*k*) long-term finance by ECGD financial guarantees or in co-operation with international bodies such as the World Bank.
A word about each of these is now desirable.

6.2 Financing export trade from capital

When a firm carries on business in the home trade, it usually gives its customers one month's credit and the time-lag between delivery of the goods or services and payment for them is carried as a normal expense of business, financed by the use of the firm's own capital. When a firm embarks upon overseas trade the time-lag may be longer and the difficulty of financing the export activity is increased. One way to finance the export activity is to obtain more capital by a new issue of shares. Alternatively, an issue of debentures, which are loans to the company, may be made. It depends entirely upon the situation of the business as to whether this is a desirable policy. If shares are issued, they will, of course, have to earn a dividend, either a fixed dividend in the case of preference shares, or a share of the total available dividend in the case of ordinary shares. Shares are also likely to carry with them some sort of voting interest, which may affect control of the company. If debentures are issued, they will need to be paid an agreed rate of interest. The holders will also often have some sort of recourse against the assets of the company if the interest payment is not forthcoming. There are therefore two problems in each case: how the necessary dividend or interest money will be found, and what the implications of a new issue of shares or debentures are for the conduct of the company.

This method of financing has several advantages. For instance, it usually means that the export activity is financed at a known cost (the preference dividend, the debenture rate of interest or the usual distribution made to ordinary shareholders), the company is not at the mercy of volatile interest rates, as it is when borrowing from a bank, and provided the export activity can be conducted profitably, it will usually be safe to finance trade in this way.

6.3 Financing by overdraft or bank loan facilities

Overdrafts and bank loans are, of course, available to all sound businesses and, if they are arranged to promote the conduct of export businesses, the usual safeguards will be required by the bank. This means that some sort of collateral security must be provided, for example the deeds of property must be surrendered or some sort of debenture on the fixed or floating (stock) assets must be agreed. The whole financial position of the company must also be subjected to appraisal by the bank granting the loan. Interest at between 2 and 5 per cent above the bank base rate must also be paid. Giving security against the general assets of the business is clearly undesirable from the exporter's point of view, and such arrangements are less satisfactory than a method of finance more directly linked to the export transactions themselves.

In the commodity markets loans are often raised against the security of the commodities that are being traded. The security takes the form of a pledge of the commodities, giving actual or constructive possession of the goods. Constructive possession is gained by the possession of the documents endorsed in blank (see explanation in section 5.1.2). Documents endorsed in this way (whether they are bills of lading or negotiable warehouse documents) give the bank the right to take possession of the goods. The bank will also require a letter of hypothecation (see section 5.5.2) giving it the right to resell the goods in the event of any default.

Finance arranged against the security of goods in this way has the advantage of leaving the ordinary assets of a company unaffected.

6.4 Finance by negotiation

Finance by negotiation amounts to the purchase by the bank of the exporter's bill drawn on the foreign customer (see also sections 4.5.1 and 4.8.6). The full value of the bill is advanced to the exporter, and the remitting banker sends the bill for collection for its own account. If the foreign importer has expressed willingness to pay the interest charges, these will be collected on behalf of the negotiating banker; if there is any question of non-payment, the negotiating banker will debit its customer's (i.e. the exporter's) account with the full value of the bill and the interest due.

6.5 Finance from advances against collections

When a bank does not wish to advance the full face value of a bill (i.e. negotiate it) or when an exporter can finance a proportion of the credit it is giving the importer out of its own funds, it is usual to take out a loan secured on the collection proceeds for the amount desired. This requires the exporter to pledge the proceeds of the bill against the advance made, so that the advance and the interest are deducted from the sum collected; only the balance is paid to the exporter. The pledge takes the form of a letter of pledge entitling the bank to recover the advance plus interest from the proceeds of any bills held on the exporter's behalf. The bank is not a party to the bill, but has a lien on the proceeds until all sums to which it is entitled have been recovered.

In certain circumstances the bank may require the exporter to give a general letter of hypothecation to cover the right to sell the goods, and not just pledge the bill, if it is a documentary collection, while the availability of ECGD cover (see section 6.7) will usually persuade a bank to grant a loan.

6.6 Finance by acceptance credits

An acceptance credit is a credit made available to an exporter against the security of documents and drafts lodged for collection with and pledged to a merchant bank. The credit is usually for an agreed proportion of the value of the collection (say, 80 per cent). The exporter draws on the bank, giving a date for maturity rather longer than the credit period given to the importer. The bank then accepts the bill he draws and discounts it with a discount house. Because it bears the name of a reputable bank, the bill is discounted at a good rate. The sum realised is paid to the exporter, less a small 'acceptance' charge of about 1 per cent per annum.

This method of raising finance is cheaper than an ordinary overdraft facility, since the discounting rate plus the charge made by the bank together come to less than the 2 per cent above bank base rate often charged by the commercial banks for a loan. On the due date the bill will be presented to the bank by the 'holder in due course', whoever he may be. The bank honours the bill, but by that time the proceeds of the collection should be available to cover the sum due, any balance being paid to the exporter.

6.7 Financing by advances secured on an ECGD guarantee

The Export Credits Guarantee Department is a specialist government department which insures a variety of risks encountered in the export trade. These risks are usually the most difficult to insure in the ordinary insurance markets, often because they are not easily calculated. In the course of nearly half a century of operations the ECGD has accumulated a vast background knowledge of foreign trading organisations. This enables it to give sound opinions on the reliability of customers. The reader should note that it is always desirable to give the expected level of business to be conducted: a customer who is sound at £5,000 per year may be less suitable to deal with at £50,000 a year and totally unacceptable if he is proposing to place orders for £500,000. An indication from the ECGD that they are not prepared to offer cover at the level proposed is a clear sign that the customer is over-reaching himself. The insolvency of the buyer is one of several headings for which it is possible to obtain cover from the Export Credits Guarantee Department. These insurance policies are described in detail in Chapter 8.

The normal ECGD policy covers an exporter against losses up to about 90 per cent, or sometimes 95 per cent, of invoice price. For a small extra premium the Department will give a direct guarantee to the exporter's bank for 100 per cent of the finance provided. The Department agrees a revolving credit limit for the finance it will guarantee, and the exporter pays the premium, which is at a very small percentage of the agreed limit (currently $\frac{1}{4}$ per cent per annum). There are two possible schemes. The Comprehensive Bill Guarantee is used when there are bills of exchange being drawn upon the customer by the exporter, or promissory notes being given by the customer to the exporter. The exporter lodges these with his bank, together with the shipping documents or buyer's certificate of performance in the case of services, and a standard form of warranty that his ECGD policy is in order. He is then given finance at a lower rate of interest ($\frac{5}{8}$ per cent above base rate). In the event of non-payment the bank is reimbursed with interest by the ECGD. The Department reserves a right of recourse against the exporter for the small part of the funds it has had to pay to the bank which it would not have had to pay to the exporter – because he was only insured for 90 per cent (or 95 per cent).

The Comprehensive Open-account Guarantee is very similar. There is often, of course, no bill of exchange or promissory note from the customer in 'open account' dealing. Instead, the exporter makes out a promissory note to his bank, which grants him a loan of 90 per cent of the invoice price. The exporter is thus promising to honour the note on the due date. If he does not, the ECGD honours the note with the bank, and recovers from the exporter. In normal circumstances the customer, who is paying the exporter direct, will pay the debt in due course and enable the exporter to honour his promissory note without difficulty.

6.8 Non-recourse finance by an export finance house

Non-recourse finance is finance which is given to the exporter's overseas buyer by a finance house which acquires no rights to claim repayment from the exporter, should the payment from the foreign customer not materialise, except for the obvious implications of warranty of performance by the exporter. This puts the exporter in the position of a seller for cash. The finance house will arrange contractually with the foreign customer for satisfaction of the debt. Clearly they will offer this service only after careful investigation as to the foreign buyer's creditworthiness, and will usually obtain credit insurance under their own ECGD policy. Once this is complete they will give the exporter a contract of confirmation which ensures payment against specified shipping documents in good order. Frequently copy documents are good enough for this purpose since the finance house only requires proof that the exporter has done what he promised to do. The actual documents can be sent direct to the foreign importer, who has been thoroughly vetted for creditworthiness. If any default occurs, the finance house will pursue its contractual rights against the foreign buyer (debtor), aware, of course, that it must properly represent the best interests of ECGD, who may well be called upon to pay a claim if the default is protracted.

A large UK export finance house such as Barclays Export Services Ltd liaises directly with the foreign importer, often through its associated banks and representatives. It is able to offer home exporters a sophisticated payments service against presentation of documents, and foreign importers a short- and/or medium-term credit facility against promissory notes in line with the terms of trade appropriate to the underlying sales contract. A finance house can often offer longer periods of credit than an ordinary exporter.

6.9 Finance by factoring

Factoring is a procedure whereby a specialist company – the factoring company – takes over the debtors' ledger (sales ledger) of a firm, and for an agreed fee assumes responsibility for the accounting records, invoicing and collection of payments due. The factoring company usually expects to take over both home and overseas accounts, with a turnover of at least £50,000 per year. It exercises credit control, lodges documents against payment or acceptance, deals with forward exchange transactions and generally relieves the exporter of many difficulties connected with overseas trade. It will advance money against outstanding payments up to about 80 per cent, charging market rates of interest. Since a factoring company may act for a number of firms it can clearly achieve economies in the account supervision, credit control and debt collection fields. It usually has a network of home and overseas agents able to follow up bad debtors and achieve debt collection without many of the dificulties which would face the exporter.

The nine major factoring companies are members of the Association of British Factors, which is based at Moor House, London Wall, London EC2Y 5HE. Factoring companies can usually also offer the facility of 'invoice discounting' (see below).

6.10 Finance by invoice discounting

A rather similar activity to factoring is invoice discounting. It is used where an export house acts as neither a merchant house nor a confirming house but only as an agent for the foreign importer or the United Kingdom exporter. The actual contract lies directly between the importer and exporter. In these circumstances the export house may agree to discount the invoices to the exporter, giving him immediate payment of part of the value as an advance. The charge is a flat rate for the period of credit envisaged to the importer. In the event of non-payment the export house has a right of recourse against the exporter, but will usually extend the advance on payment of a further charge. The export house does not usually collect debts; it is for the exporter to secure payment from the customer.

6.11 Medium-term finance

In international trade medium-term finance means finance lasting for between two and five years. This type of finance is provided in two ways.

The first method is by loans from the commercial banks to either the supplier or the buyer, and secured against an ECGD guarantee. These guarantees are called Specific Guarantees (for supplier credit) and Buyer Credit Guarantees, the latter being given only for orders of capital goods in excess of £250,000.

To provide security for the Department the exporter will draw bills of exchange to cover the repayments with interest, usually at six-monthly intervals; with Buyer Credit Guarantees the buyer will provide promissory notes in the same way. A promissory note is similar in effect to a bill of exchange, but instead of the drawer drawing upon a drawee, who becomes the acceptor of the bill and liable upon it, the promissor writes the note and promises to pay the money himself. An ordinary banknote is a promissory note. The ECGD who is supplying without recourse finance to the exporter has in both cases a document which must be honoured, and can be protested for dishonour to the importer's great discredit if it is not met on the due date.

The second method of providing finance is by 'lines of credit'. A line of credit is an ECGD guarantee on a sterling loan made by a British bank to an overseas government, or government agency, or even to a private sector institution. The loan period, and the types of goods it is issued to finance, are specified. The loan agreement supplies 80 per cent of the finance required for the project, the other 20 per cent, including a substantial down payment, is paid by the foreign customer. The British exporters are paid in cash, and the foreign importer benefits because he is able to secure better credit terms since he is negotiating finance for a large number of orders. Lines of credit are announced in *British Business* and in such trade magazines as Croner's *Export Digest* which is sent free to those who use the *Reference Book for Exporters*. A typical announcement would read as follows.

The Export Credits Guarantee Department has guaranteed a £5 million line of credit which Lloyds Bank International Ltd has made available to Privredna Banka, Zagreb, Yugoslavia. The loan will help finance contracts placed in the UK for capital goods and associated services by Yugoslavian buyers. UK exporters will receive 85 per cent of the contract price from the loan after shipment of the goods; the remaining 15 per cent is payable from the buyer's own resources.

To qualify under the terms of the loan a contract must have a minimum value of £10,000 and be placed by 30 September 19...

Exporters interested in further details of this facility should contact. . . . .

6.12 Long-term finance

Very long-term finance is usually arranged by special international bodies, such as the International Bank for Reconstruction and Development (IBRD), or under the UK bilateral aid agreements. Exporters who supply goods and services for such projects are paid in cash, without recourse, the 'aid' organisation taking full responsibility for securing repayments from the importer.

The ECGD will also consider long-term guarantees for loans exceeding a five-year repayment period on certain types of capital goods projects. The aim of these loan guarantees is to enable British exporters to compete with foreign suppliers who are using long-term credit to achieve unfair advantage in a particular market. Continuous monitoring of long-term contracts reported under the exchange of information systems between members of the Berne Union identifies problem areas and the ECGD endeavours to match the situation of British exporters with competitors, to ensure that they are not adversely affected by long-term credit competition.

6.13 Bank finance for imports

In a free-trade system, or in a limited free-trade system such as that prevailing within a free-trade area, import trade must be increasingly common. The pattern of United Kingdom import trade in recent years shows a huge increase in imports of semi-manufactured and manufactured goods.

Bank finance for imports may be obtained in the following ways.

6.13.1 *Overdrafts and loans*

Where the importer is believed to be absolutely reliable, an unsecured overdraft or loan may be made available to meet regular commitments or occasional transactions. Any security taken may be unrelated to the goods in question, and it is usually based on the importer's fixed assets or stocks generally. Although the bank relies generally on the known creditworthiness of its customer, the importer should show good faith by paying the proceeds from any particular importing transaction into the account to offset (i.e. reduce) the overdraft or loan, so that the series of transactions is self-liquidating.

6.13.2 *Produce loans*

Some importers dealing in basic commodities which are normally carried in bulk may be involved in transactions of far greater value than their own capital resources, so that security for a loan would not be possible from the capital assets that they own personally. In such cases the loan will be secured against the produce itself, but it will not usually be for the full value of the produce, a varying margin being allowed depending on the circumstances. Thus, where goods are pre-sold to a buyer of undoubted integrity the margin may be quite small, but where the deal is speculative, or the market fluctuates considerably, or there are storage risks and costs to be borne the loan will be reduced accordingly. The security for the loan is the shipping documents for goods in transit, and the goods themselves on arrival. If the goods have to be released to the importer for delivery to a buyer, a trust receipt is usually taken to ensure that the proceeds of the sale are paid to the bank for credit against the loan account within a limited period (usually a few days).

6.13.3 *Other methods*

Some of the methods already described in the export sections of this book may be employed to provide finance for the importer. Thus, a clean acceptance credit facility may be used to help an importer who is required to pay for goods on arrival but unable to collect payment from his eventual customer. A bill drawn on the bank for acceptance by them will be discounted and the proceeds used to pay for the goods on arrival. By the time this bill falls due the proceeds from the sale of the goods should bc available to honour the bill. Similarly, finance houses, like Barclays Export Services Ltd, can provide finance to importers, meeting the foreign supplier's requirements in full on shipment. The finance is made available as a line of credit for terms ranging from 60 days to 2 years, according to the nature of the goods and the custom of the trade.

6.14 Summary of Chapter 6

1. The problem of financing overseas trade is one of bridging the gap between the making of a contract and the receipt of payment for performing it.
2. Export trade can be financed out of ordinary capital, or loans from debenture holders. Alternatively, normal overdraft or bank loan facilities may be used.
3. Short-term finance can be obtained in several ways: by negotiating bills of exchange drawn upon a customer, by arranging an advance against bills sent for collections, or by arranging an acceptance credit for a large percentage of the sum receivable from the foreign customer, to mature at a slightly later date, in which case the foreign customer's payment should arrive in time to honour the acceptance when it falls due. A fourth way is by arranging a bank advance against an ECGD Comprehensive Bill Guarantee or Comprehensive Open-account Guarantee.
4. Export finance houses provide finance to the export trade by assisting creditworthy foreign customers. The exporter is paid in cash, without recourse, the finance house looking to the security of its own arrangements with the foreign customer backed by its own ECGD policy of credit insurance.
5. Factoring is a means of providing finance by surrending the conduct of the sales ledger to a specialist factoring company, which establishes its own system of credit control and debt collection. Invoice discounting works in a similar way.
6. Medium- and long-term finance tends to be provided by ECGD guarantees to banks making loans on specific capital projects, or against 'lines of credit' opened up by ECGD to foreign governments or government agencies.

6.15 Questions on Chapter 6

1. What is meant by the term 'financing foreign trade'? How may finance be provided for (*a*) short-term and (*b*) medium-term contracts?
2. 'Export trade is only an extension of home trading, and ideally should be financed out of the ordinary capital of the business.' Discuss the arguments for and against this type of finance for overseas trade.
3. What is a 'London acceptance credit'? How is it useful to a businessman in need of finance?
4. What is meant by 'negotiation' in the special circumstances of export trade? Explain in detail how the system works.
5. What is meant by 'without recourse' finance? If an export finance house offers without recourse finance to a United Kingdom exporter, to whom will it look for satsifaction in the event of non-payment and how will it safeguard its position?
6. What is 'factoring'? How may it benefit an exporter? Are there any disadvantages?
7. Explain at least three of the following:
   (*a*) line of credit,
   (*b*) London acceptance credit,
   (*c*) advances against collections,
   (*d*) negotiation,
   (*e*) letter of hypothecation,
   (*f*) credit factoring,
   (*g*) invoice discounting.

Chapter 7
Other methods of overseas trade

7.1 Trading on consignment terms

The essence of consignment trading is that goods exported on consignment remain the property of the United Kingdom exporter, and are sold for him by an agent who then renders an account called an 'account sales'. The goods concerned are effectively stock located in a different position from the exporter's home warehouse. The overseas agent is advised of the stock being sent to him by means of a pro forma invoice. This gives him some idea of the price the exporter hopes to realise when the goods are sold. Any expenses incurred, such as handling charges, warehousing, insurance and auctioneer's or selling expenses, are for the exporter's account. When goods are sold the agent will render an account sales which shows the gross proceeds, the expenses incurred and the agent's commission. The agent may in addition act as a *del credere* agent. *Del credere* means 'in the belief that' and implies that the agent acts 'in the belief that the buyer is solvent'. Because a *del credere* agent believes that the buyer is solvent, he is prepared to run the risk of any bad debts that may occur, and for this he is paid an extra commission. Clearly, the agent has a far better chance of pursuing a bad debtor successfully than the exporter, who is thus relieved of possible bad debts. The account sales is usually accompanied by a sight draft for the net proceeds of the transaction.

With commodities such as bulk raw materials a similar procedure is followed. The goods are shipped in bulk to an independent agent such as a bank, which is authorised to permit named brokers in the commodity concerned to inspect and sample the product. The goods are warehoused, insured and delivered to any broker against orders for a specified quantity for which he is prepared to pay. The bank will then render an account sales and the net proceeds to the exporter. A typical account sales is shown in Figure 7.1.

Account sales
By M. Dobbs & Co.
70 St Mary Axe
Sydney
Australia

To Easifreeze Ltd
20 High Street
Camside
England

1 April 19. .

In the matter of 280 Easifreeze refrigerators sold ex SS Golden Ray by your order at best price obtainable.

		A$
280 × A$158.50		= 44 380.00
Charges:	A$	
Landing charges	384.50	
Warehousing	465.00	
Insurance	248.00	
Auctioneer's expenses	409.95	
Brokerage at $1\frac{1}{4}\%$	554.75	
Commission at $2\frac{1}{2}\%$	1 109.50	
Del credere	443.80	
		3 615.50
		A$40 764.50
Converted at A$1.6738 = £1 Sight draft enclosed		£24 354.46

Figure 7.1 An account sales.

7.2 Joint ventures

A joint venture is a type of partnership for a limited period in which two or more parties engage in trade for the purpose of disposing of a particular batch of goods. Generally the parties concerned have different kinds of expertise which are necessary to the contract, for example one might be particularly knowledgeable about buying and another about selling, or one might be able to obtain (or manufacture) particular types of equipment, but not know who needs this type of equipment or how to establish links with a particular class of customer separated by language barriers, religious customs, etc.

The essence of joint venture is that each party bears the expenses that occur in his particular activity, charging the costs to a joint venture account in his own books. Each party also receives whatever proceeds there are at his particular level and credits these to the joint venture account in his own books. Frequently, most of the costs will accrue to one of the parties and most of the proceeds will be received by the other.

At the end of the activities each will send the other a copy of his joint venture account and from the two accounts a memorandum joint venture account can be prepared. The profit can thus be calculated and divided in the agreed way. The one with most of the money will now retain his share of the profit and his share of the expenses and send to the other the remainder, which will be the other's share of the profit and his share of the expenses. An imaginary set of accounts is shown in Table 7.1 to illustrate the system.

Table 7.1
(*a*) Joint venture account in the books of Thomas Mann (Royston) Ltd

19 . .		£	19 . .		£
Jan. 31	Raw materials	7 850.00	Mar. 31	Refund of fees paid	17.50
31	Labour	3 260.00			
Feb. 12	Packing, etc.	854.00			
14	Shipping charges	1 574.50			

(*b*) Joint venture account in the books of Abdullah (Lagos) Ltd

19 . .		£	19 . .		£
Mar. 12	Warehousing	275.80	Apr. 1	Gross proceeds	42 565.00
12	Insurance	384.50			
17	Auction expenses	352.50			
Apr. 1	Commission	851.30			

When the records shown in Table 7.1 are matched, it is possible to calculate the profit figure, which is shared two-thirds to Thomas Mann (Royston) Ltd and one-third to Abdullah (Lagos) Ltd (see Table 7.2).

The amount due to Mann from Abdullah is then found as follows: Abdullah's profit, £9,059.97, is entered on the left-hand side of the joint venture account in his books, making the total on that side on his account come to £10,924.07. When this is deducted from the gross proceeds it leaves £31,640.93, which is the amount that he must send to Thomas Mann (Royston) Ltd. When the sight draft arrives it will cover all Mann's expenses (£13,538.50 – £17.50 = £13,521.00) plus the profit due to Mann of £18,119.93. Both parties have therefore recovered their expenses and a considerable profit on the transaction.

In the above example no attempt has been made to show such matters as the use of different currencies in the two countries, but it is clear that this will involve only a relatively minor adjustment in the accounts.

Table 7.2 Memorandum joint venture account Mann and Abdullah

			£				£
19 . .				19 . .			
Jan.	31	Raw materials	7 850.00	Mar.	31	Refund of fees paid	17.50
	31	Labour	3 260.00	Apr.	1	Gross proceeds	42 565.00
							42 582.50
Feb.	12	Packing, etc.	854.00				
	14	Shipping charges	1 574.50				
Mar.	12	Warehousing	275.80				
	12	Insurance	384.50				
	17	Auction expenses	352.50				
Apr.	1	Commission	851.30				
			15 402.60				
		Profit	27 179.90				
			£42 582.50				£42 582.50
		Profit to Mann	18 119.93			Profit	27 179.90
		Profit to Abdullah	9 059.97				

7.3 Participation agreements

Many developing countries seek to ensure the participation of their own nationals in international trading activities by insisting that expatriates are admitted only to the extent that they are prepared to share the fruits of the enterprise with home nationals. This may be done by co-operating with a local firm in the same line of business or setting up a joint company with directors who are nationals of the country concerned. Co-operation in this way is clearly highly desirable: the company is seen to be beneficial and plays a positive part in developing the expertise and business skill of the local staff. The Overseas Trade Divisions of the Department of Trade can assist with advice about restrictions of this sort imposed by foreign governments, and with the names of likely companies prepared to consider participation schemes.

7.4 Licensing the use of know-how: royalty agreements

Rather similar to the participation agreements referred to above are the licensing arrangements made with foreign firms for the exploitation of patent processes and techniques. The royalty payments become an invisible export. Instead of manufacturing a product and shipping it to the export market, a contract is drawn up for the use of a particular process or even for the construction of a complete industrial complex, with a royalty on output as the eventual long-term result. Clearly, such projects can be very large-scale activities and may need the development of a consortium to push them through. Care is necessary when framing the royalty agreement. It is usual to fix a 'minimum rent' below which the royalty cannot fall, even if output does not justify it on a piecework basis. When the output rises above that necessary to earn the minimum rent, the royalty based on this total output is payable. Sometimes the payment of a minimum rent in the early years can be recouped by the licensee in subsequent years when output does rise above the minimum rent position.

7.5 Bilateral trading

Certain countries, particularly the COMECON countries of the Eastern Bloc and the developing countries of Africa and South America, are prepared to trade only on a bilateral basis. This has been explained earlier (see page 26) and means that purchases from an advanced nation must be compensated by an equal purchase of goods from the developing nation. Whether this is acceptable depends upon the products being offered by the country concerned and the degree of opposition likely to be aroused in the home country by the goods being imported. Thus, the shoe trade is at present most unhappy about foreign shoes being unloaded in this country in the course of East–West trade.

Such difficulties arise because of limitations on the free workings of foreign exchange markets and of interference with normal methods of settling indebtedness. Some economists call this the 'funny money' business. The exporter may be paid in currency which can only be spent in the country to which he exported his goods. He may be paid in a currency which may be spent in one or two places, but is not convertible otherwise. He may be expected to accept in exchange goods of a specified type and at an agreed price, whether he agrees with that price as fair or not. He may even be expected to wait until the factory he has helped to build is actually producing, and then to take some of the output as his share. This has certainly been the case with at least one automobile plant built in the Eastern Bloc countries. In many cases these arrangements are acceptable, but bearing in mind the sophisticated nature of the negotiating personnel on the state-trading side, it can mean a period of very tough bargaining before the agreement is concluded.

The expertise which exists in a free enterprise economy has produced specialist dealers in this particular field who are sometimes called 'barter and switch' experts. Like all brokers, they specialise in knowing who wants what and who has got what, and by bringing the two parties into contact they divert goods received in such deals to places where they can be disposed of favourably.

Where communist countries do enter the market with foreign exchange to spend, which means that a firm decision has been taken to apply a proportion of the national income to the purchase of a particular product, there are no payment difficulties. Payment is made 45 days after delivery and no bills of exchange are handled. An exporter requiring short-term finance would therefore need to rely on his normal banking arrangements, but for medium-term finance ECGD backing would be available on a specific policy relating to and reflecting the risks involved in that particular contract.

7.6 Trust receipts

The availability of goods is sometimes restricted, for example they may have been pledged to a bank as security for a loan. If this is the case and the customer wishes to obtain the goods in order to sell them, he will be required to sign a *trust receipt*, which acknowledges that he takes possession of the goods as trustee for the bank, and will deal with them only as trustee. This means that he will warehouse them in a named independent warehouse, or will manufacture them and then warehouse them in a named warehouse. If disposed of to a named purchaser, the proceeds will be paid without deduction to the bank so that they can be used to extinguish a loan, the balance being paid to the exporter's account.

This procedure is not without its risks for the bank. It has the safeguard that if the customer gets into financial difficulties the trust receipt is evidence that the goods are not the property of the customer, and cannot be taken over by a liquidator or trustee in bankruptcy. On the other hand, a customer who fails to honour the trust receipt and sells the goods to a third party does give the third party a valid title to the goods, leaving the bank to pursue its customer to recover what it can (if it can find him).

7.7 Indemnities

Indemnity arises in any circumstances where the action of one party may result in a loss to another party. Thus, where a ship has arrived but a bill of lading has not, the importer claiming the goods may be prepared to give an idemnity usually also involving his bank to the shipowner to release the goods. Should any third party bring an action against the shipowner for failure to deliver the goods when presented with the bill of lading, the importer will indemnify the shipowner for any losses suffered.

A similar case is where a letter of credit calls for 'clean bills of lading', but only a dirty bill, claused by the shipowner, is available. An indemnity covering the derogatory clause may be entered into. Care must, however, be taken not to overstep the bounds of reasonable behaviour as far as indemnities are concerned. In one case – *Brown Jenkinson & Co. Ltd* v. *Percy Dalton (London) Ltd* (1930) – the defendants gave an indemnity not against the existence of a derogatory clause but against the issue of a clean bill of lading when manifest damage had been sustained by the cargo, which deceived the eventual purchaser into thinking he was buying goods that were undamaged. The parties were held to have intended to deceive, although they did not intend that the eventual purchaser would ultimately go without compensation.

7.8 Summary of Chapter 7

1. Trading on consignment terms involves sending goods to overseas agents who sell them for the best price obtainable and remit the net proceeds. Joint ventures are a similar arrangement, but the relationship is one of temporary partnership rather than agency. Profits on the venture are shared in some agreed manner.
2. Participation agreements and licensing arrangements are acceptable methods of exporting, particularly to countries where national aspirations aim at the development of local personnel as part of a general development programme.
3. Trade with communist countries and certain developing coun-

tries is carried on mainly through state trading corporations. Barter and other arrangements may be necessary where shortage of foreign exchange is a problem.

4. In the sophisticated affairs of businessmen such devices as trust receipts and indemnities may be developed to lend confidence to one party in a particular transaction so that goods can be freed to proceed to their ultimate destination.

7.9 Questions on Chapter 7

1. What is an 'account sales'? What types of charges are likely to be listed on such an account?
2. What are the exporting problems of developing countries? How may they be made to feel that trade is mutually beneficial?
3. What are 'barter' arrangements? Why are these arrangements commonly made with communist countries? What difficulties may be encountered?
4. What is an indemnity? In what circumstances might a letter of indemnity be used to promote the freer movement of goods?
5. What is a trust receipt? How may it be used to secure the release of goods immobilised by a pledge as security for a loan?
6. X Ltd are manufacturers of quality furniture. Hassan is an arab trader specialising in western goods for the Middle East market. How may they pursue mutually advantageous trading relationships where Islamic rejection of any type of usury is taken into account?

Chapter 8
Export credit guarantees

8.1 The Export Credits Guarantee Department

The Export Credits Guarantee Department is a Government Department which was set up in 1930 to offer insurance for export credits on headings where ordinary insurance was not available. In one recent year it paid out about £300 million in claims, about 70 per cent of which was for losses caused by non-buyer risks; the other 30 per cent arose from the insolvency or default of buyers. The Department has sophisticated information services, which enable it to anticipate adverse trends in any particular area and take action to minimise risks. As a result its average charge for cover of short-term risks is low, though it has risen during the recent years of recession.

The Department assists exporters in two ways. First, it insures them against the risk of non-payment, through the fault of the buyer or for any other reason. Secondly, by offering unconditional guarantees of 100 per cent repayment to banks, it encourages them to offer credit to exporters at favourable rates of interest. This is a service which for some reason is not widely appreciated by exporters. So many firms think of ECGD only in terms of insurance against bad debts and overlook its services as guarantor when they borrow from the banks themselves. The Department acts on a commercial basis, seeking to cover its losses by its premium receipts and to date has managed to operate without any burden falling upon the Exchequer. It draws its powers from the Export Guarantees Acts 1968 and 1970. Under Section 1 of the 1968 Act the Department's activities relate to purely commercial business which forms 90 per cent of its work. The remaining 10 per cent, under Section 11 of the Act, relates to insurance cover of a non-commercial nature granted as a public service in the national interest. Because of its entrenched position in the international trade scene, the Department is able to make recoveries in some cases many years after the loss occurred, when the financial climate in the country concerned improves, and long after other insurance companies might have been forced to relinquish an interest in overdue accounts. Under a further Act, the Overseas Investment and Export Guarantees Act 1972, the Department offers cover for new investment overseas against expropriation, war or restriction on remittances. This type of cover is outside the area of the Foundation Course in Overseas Trade.

In fixing its premiums ECGD has to strike three balances.

(*a*) It must not incur losses, taking one year with another, so that premiums must be high enough to avoid burdening the Exchequer.
(*b*) It avoids surpluses, other than those needed to establish sound reserves over the years, bearing in mind the rising volume of cover being offered.
(*c*) It must deal fairly between customers and avoid subsidising one at the expense of another.

8.2 Types of ECGD policy

There are many types of policy available but they may be divided into two chief categories as follows.

(*a*) Comprehensive policies covering short-term trade of a repetitive type, involving standard types of goods.
(*b*) Specific policies, which cover non-repetitive trade such as contracts for civil engineering projects, large-scale capital goods items and other projects where high costs make long-term credit an essential part of the contract.

8.2.1 *Comprehensive policies*

With comprehensive policies (also called comprehensive short-term guarantees) the exporter offers most or all of his business for cover in both good and bad markets of the world. The types of cover offered are listed in Table 8.1. The exporter undertakes to insure all his export turnover for a period of at least one year, in all markets. If he elects to cover only some markets, this will be acceptable so long as they offer a reasonable spread of risks, but naturally the premium will be higher. Continuous cover is offered subject to an annual review procedure for all the agreed goods shipped overseas and can be extended to include pre-shipment cover, provided the goods are to be shipped within twelve months. These risks are called 'pre-credit' risks, and must cover all the insured export turnover, not just particular contracts. The importer should be unaware of ECGD cover.

Table 8.1 ECGD comprehensive short-term guarantees on consumer goods

Cover offered for	Percentage payable	When payable
(i) Insolvency of the buyer	90% of the loss	On proof of insolvency
(ii) Protracted default (failure to pay within six months)	90% of the loss	Six months after delivery of goods
(iii) Buyer's refusal to take delivery	90% of the remaining loss after the exporter has born 20% of the loss himself	One month after re-sale of the goods
(iv) General moratorium on foreign debt decreed by government of buyer's country	95% of the loss (90% only if goods not yet shipped)	Four months after event which causes loss, or immediately after the loss itself, whichever is later
(v) Any other government action to prevent payment	As in (iv) above	As in (iv) above
(vi) Political events, economic, administrative or legislative measures outside UK preventing transfer of funds	As in (iv) above	Four months after the due date or after the completion of the transfer, whichever is later
(vii) Legal discharge of debt in a foreign currency resulting in a shortfall	As in (iv) above	As in (vi) above
(viii) War or other frustrating event not insurable commercially	As in (iv) above	As in (iv) above
(ix) Cancellation of UK export licence (only given where the risk is covered from the time of the original contract)	As in (iv) above	As in (iv) above
(x) Repudiation of contract by a state buyer	As in (iv) above	As in (iv) above

Note: Cover does alter from time to time and the ECGD current booklet should be consulted for exact details.

Comprehensive short-term guarantees are arranged within discretionary limits without the ECGD being notified about particular consignments. A first order of up to £250 in value can be proceeded with freely provided there is no adverse information about the buyer. From £250 to £5,000 the exporter may proceed provided he has a favourable report from a bank or credit information service. Above £5,000 the ECGD will approve a credit limit. In the majority of cases therefore ECGD will become aware of a particular consignment only if payment difficulties arise.

Premiums on comprehensive policies are paid in parts. A non-refundable premium is paid as a lump sum annually in advance, and for those with an annual export turnover of less than £25,000 this is the only premium payable. For those with larger turnovers it is necessary to declare export totals monthly, when a further premium will be charged. Where pre-credit risks have to be assumed, new contracts are also declared monthly and a premium is then charged so that cover can commence.

8.2.2 *Specific policies*

With specific policies the cover is given as a tailor-made guarantee after individual negotiation between the exporter and the ECGD. Specific guarantees usually provide cover from the date of the contract, because of lengthy manufacturing periods for purpose-built equipment. Cover extends for up to five years, but extended terms cover may be available in certain circumstances, for example to meet foreign competition.

As negotiations move towards the establishment of a firm contract the ECGD makes a formal offer of cover which remains open for three months. Acceptance of this offer, and payment of the premium of between £2.25 and £4.75 per £100 (according to the market concerned) leads to the issue of a policy. Special arrangements are made for cover affecting the sale of ships and aircraft.

8.3 The pattern of ECGD policies

Since the Export Credits Guarantee Department is operating at the very centre of international trade, offering cover where commercial insurance companies are unable to assist the exporter, its affairs are necessarily subject to the pressures of practical exporting. For this reason slight variations in the types of cover it offers, and the rates it quotes, occur from time to time. Any textbook attempting to give a picture of ECGD operations must therefore deal in general terms only. The *ECGD Services* booklet, issued free of charge by the Department and revised frequently, explains the current position, and export staff will need to read *British Business* to keep abreast of changes. The policies described in the *ECGD Services* booklet are as follows.

Overseas investment insurance scheme Since the Export Guarantees and Overseas Investment Act 1978, the ECGD has offered investment cover to United Kingdom investors. Cover is provided for new overseas investment for a maximum of 15 years against political risks. The minimum period is three years, and investors must be companies carrying on business in the United Kingdom, or a subsidiary of such a company. Political risks include expropriation, war and restriction on remittances. Cover is *not* provided against the *commercial* risks of any venture overseas.

Services guarantees – comprehensive and specific cover Invisible earnings are just as vulnerable to the difficulties of international trade as 'visible' transactions. Payments for repairs, technical or professional assistance, licence and royalty payments, etc., are affected by insolvency of the customer, regulations on transfer of payments and so on. Cover for these risks is offered under 'comprehensive' policies similar to the policies offered on 'visible' sales. If a service is of a one-off nature, as where a quantity surveyor supervises the charges for a particular repair job, cover is on a 'specific' basis.

Subsidiaries guarantees Where an exporter sells goods to a subsidiary company, which then sells them to customers abroad, the Department offers cover to the subsidiary subject to certain rules. One of these rules is that they will cover the further sale only if they have already covered the sale to the subsidiary. Extended terms guarantees are also available if required.

Supplementary stocks guarantees An exporter who is selling goods from stocks established in a foreign country may be subject to losses such as war risk losses, or expropriation, requisitioning and confiscation of goods. These risks are covered by a supplementary stocks guarantee, but a level of stocks to be held has to be agreed with the Department, although it may be raised at any time by prior consultation.

External trade guarantees Some merchants, confirming houses and manufacturers use their expertise to assist foreign customers in purchasing goods from suppliers who are not UK firms. Thus a Nigerian customer might use a UK confirming house to purchase German cars. The goods would not pass through the United Kingdom but risks are still being run by UK firms and commissions or profits earned of benefit to the UK balance of payments. This type of trade can be covered by ECGD policies very similar to the comprehensive short-term guarantees described earlier. There is a small list of 'sensitive' products which enter directly into competition with UK goods for which cover is not offered.

Extended terms guarantees These are made available to those whose export turnover is covered by a normal comprehensive short-term guarantee, but who, because of the nature of the trade, require to offer a period of longer-term credit to customers as an inducement. It is offered in cases where the credit period is normally more than six months but less than five years.

Constructional works guarantees Constructional works involve the provision of goods and services. The buyer is termed 'the employer' in these guarantees, which are negotiated within the terms of an agreed code of international practice called the Conditions of Contract (International). Cover is provided on the basis of sums due on the contract, against insolvency of the employer, failure to pay within six months of sums being declared 'due', moratorium on external debts of the country or any other action by the government of the employer's country . It could also apply where sums are due because of political, economic, legislative or administrative measures, currency shortfalls, war and certain other events and cancellation of a UK export licence. If the employer is a public body and it fails to perform its part of the contract, this is covered. A supplementary contractor's plant cover is also available.

Cost-escalation cover This cover is now available to meet part of the losses sustained on long-term contracts over £5 million which are with non-EEC countries. The exporter is required to begin consultation with the Department very early in the course of the negotiations and at present cover is limited to 75 per cent on cash dealings and 70 per cent on credit dealings.

Buyer credit guarantees ECGD provides guarantees not only to exporters but also to intermediaries who are performing exporting activities on behalf of exporters (freight forwarders, for example) or are providing finance which permits credit to be granted to the foreign buyer. The bank or finance house may provide credit direct to the foreign buyer or indirectly to the foreign buyer by finance to the supplier in the United Kingdom. Buyer credit guarantees guarantee loans from banks and finance houses in the United Kingdom direct to an overseas buyer. This enables the UK exporter to be paid on cash terms, and possibly facilitates progress payments during the manufacture of large capital items, such as plant components, cranes, etc. The ECGD expects the foreign buyer to pay a substantial sum (say, 15 or 20 per cent) of the purchase price to the supplier at once, the balance being paid in full on shipment of the goods, using a loan provided to the buyer by a UK bank. The ECGD guarantees this loan for 100 per cent of the capital and interest. Early consultation is essential as four agreements have to be arranged. These are:

(*a*) a firm contract between a UK supplier and an overseas buyer for a major piece of plant or equipment and possibly their erection on site;
(*b*) a loan agreement between a financing bank in the United Kingdom and a foreign borrower, either the buyer or a bank acting on his behalf;
(*c*) an ECGD guarantee to the financing banker; and
(*d*) a premium agreement between ECGD and the UK supplier.

Supplier credit guarantees These guarantees take several forms to meet suppliers' needs for finance during the credit period which they have extended to their overseas customers. For sales with a short-term credit period (up to two years) they take two forms – the Comprehensive Bill Guarantee and the Comprehensive Open-account Guarantee. The first covers loans made by banks to exporters who have either a promissory note from the foreign importer or a bill of exchange accepted by him. Loans are made at preferential rates ($\frac{5}{8}$ per cent above base rate). Where dealings are on open account, there being no bills or promissory notes to discipline the foreign customer, the open-account guarantee to the bank covers any loan made to the exporter by the bank, pending payment by the customer.

For those requiring extended credit there is an extended terms bank guarantee on similar lines to those mentioned above.

'Lines of credit' guarantees These offer cover to United Kingdom banks giving loans to foreign buyers who wish to purchase capital items of relatively low value.

Bond support schemes Some contractors are required to give bonds (formal promises) to pay sums of money guaranteeing performance of contracts within set time-limits. Such bonds are given by banks or surety companies. The ECGD will guarantee the reimbursement of bonds paid, but claims recourse against the exporter unless he can prove that he is not at fault on the contract.

8.4 Arranging ECGD cover

ECGD cover is arranged through a number of local offices whose addresses are given in the *ECGD Services* booklet and in telephone directories. Early consultation is essential on some of the policies, for instance on long-term credit risks which must be assessed very carefully before a fair premium can be determined. Contact is best established by 'phoning the office concerned and arranging an appointment. Once an initial contact has been made, negotiations follow routine procedures and there should be little difficulty in dealing with any sort of cover required, so long as negotiations on a particular contract start in good time.

8.5 Summary of Chapter 8

1. The Export Credits Guarantee Department offers a wide range of cover to exporters likely to be adversely affected by risks caused by insolvency of the buyer, foreign exchange control regulations, deterioration of markets, wars, cost escalation and so on.
2. The two chief categories of policy are comprehensive guarantees and specific guarantees. These guarantee exporters against a variety of risks either on their total export trade or on specific contracts of a large-scale nature.
3. The usual range of cover provided includes insolvency of the buyer, protracted default (failure to pay within six months of the due date), any type of government action to prevent payment, political, economic, administrative or legislative measures, war or other frustrating event (not coverable by ordinary insurance) and cancellation of UK export licences.
4. Besides comprehensive guarantees and specific guarantees, the ECGD offers many specialist covers including overseas investment cover, services guarantees, subsidiaries guarantees, external trade guarantees, extended terms guarantees, constructional works guarantees and cost-escalation cover.
5. The ECGD also plays a major part in assisting finance for overseas trade by providing guarantees to banks and other intermediaries for buyer and supplier credit finance.

8.6 Questions on Chapter 8

1. Describe the work of the Export Credits Guarantee Department, referring particularly in your answer to the part it plays in promoting export trade.

2. Explain the nature of ECGD comprehensive short-term guarantees. For which types of trade would these policies be suitable and what is the range of covers offered?
3. The Export Credits Guarantee Department prefers that foreign importers should not know that their suppliers (the British exporters) have insured with ECGD. Why do you think this is so?
4. Write briefly about any two of the following:
   (*a*) buyer credit financing,
   (*b*) constructional works guarantees,
   (*c*) external trade guarantees,
   (*d*) cost-escalation cover,
   (*e*) extended terms guarantees,
   (*f*) comprehensive open-account guarantees.
5. What are specific policies? What types of firm need these ECGD policies and why is early consultation desirable?
6. Distinguish between an ECGD comprehensive bill guarantee and an ECGD comprehensive open-account guarantee.

Chapter 9
Sundry other matters

9.1 Organising your studies

In studying any subject it is necessary to organise yourself so that the maximum advantage is taken of the facilities available. The following suggestions will be helpful.

(*a*) There are three stages in acquiring knowledge: (*i*) the background picture; (*ii*) the detailed facts; and (*iii*) consolidation of the knowledge by written work.

(*b*) The background picture is established first of all by reading a chapter of the textbook through fairly quickly, to pick up the general line of the argument. It is also helped by the delivery of the lecturer (if you are attending a course of lectures) and your general business experience. You should enrich your background knowledge almost every day in the course of your studies and your work – a process that will continue throughout your working life.

(*c*) The detailed study requires you to make notes of the subject-matter of the chapter. Making notes is a very valuable activity, because it trains you to sort out the important facts from the descriptive material around them. Later, for example if you manage a department or a firm, it might be particularly important for you to be able to pin down the essential details of changes affecting the firm, and take action to implement plans or counter adverse trends. A good way to organise your notes is to use a lever-arch file, with index sheets made of brown paper for each chapter of the book. Then you can not only keep your notes in order, but also add to them anything else that is relevant. Examples are such items as copies of documents, newspaper articles that are relevant, reports of legal cases, essays written in answer to the questions at the ends of chapters, etc. This makes a much more interesting collection to browse through than a mere set of notes. A two-hole punch is essential to file away these notes in good order – quite satisfactory ones can be purchased very cheaply.

(*d*) Written work is essential if accuracy is to be achieved. 'Writing maketh an exact man', said Francis Bacon. If you want to make sure you know all about a particular subject, try to write a full explanation of it. Don't worry about whether anyone else will ever see it, or who is going to mark your written work. You can appraise it for yourself. If you are sure your facts are right, and you have set them down to your own satisfaction, and if your own office experience seems to bear out the understanding you have of the matter, then you will have benefited greatly from the activity. It is not too much to try every question in this book. If you do, and write a lucid answer to each one, you can be fairly confident that you will be successful in your examinations. Examinations are, of course, important, but more important are real-life situations. If you answer every question in this book, you should be able not only to pass your examinations but also to grasp the essentials of any financial problem that you encounter in international trade. More detailed reading on that particular problem can then be undertaken.

(*e*) As your examinations approach you must intensify your work. To help you through there is a checklist in section 9.2. Go through this checklist and make quite sure you have covered everything.

(*f*) Finally, there are past papers of most examinations available. It is a good idea to work through these old papers, and by all means try to answer them. More important, though, is to put yourself in the place of the examiner, and imagine yourself setting the next paper. Which parts of the syllabus are so important that an appropriate question must be devised for them? Which parts have been rather neglected in the past, so that it is high time a question was devised to test them? You should then make up two or three question papers and write answers to your own questions. When you enter the examination room you will probably find half the questions you have devised are on the paper waiting to be answered.

9.2 A checklist of examination topics

To be confident about passing an examination it is essential to feel that you have studied the syllabus fully and are thoroughly familiar with every aspect of it. Here is a checklist of every topic in the International Trade and Payments part of the Foundation Course in Overseas Trade. Tick off those items about which you feel knowledgeable. Use the index of the book to trace the others and read them up as fully as you can, and then find a relevant question in the exercises at the end of the appropriate chapter and write a detailed and formal answer for it.

The three types of economy____; The pattern of UK trade____; Sources of information on markets____; Channels of overseas trade____; Ancillary services in overseas trade____; Commodity markets____; Multinational companies____; Visible trade and invisible trade____; The balance of trade____; The balance of payments____; Bilateral trade____; Multilateral trade____; Gold standard mechanism____; Managed flexibility____; Floating exchange rates____; The International Monetary Fund ____; The International Bank for Reconstruction and Development____; General Agreement on Tariffs and Trade____; Free trade areas____; European Economic Community____; Trading with Comecon countries____; Compensation trade (barter)____; Pricing exports____; Costs of production____; Incoterms 1980 ____; Ex works____; FRC (free carrier)____; FOR/FOT____; FOA____; FAS____; FOB____; CFR____; CIF____; DCP ____; CIP____; EXS____; EXQ____; DAF____; DDP____; Import prices____; Choice of currency____; Currency baskets ____; ECU____; SDR____; Avoidance of exchange risks____; Credit management____; Methods of payment____; Cash with order____; Export house transactions____; Documentary letters of credit____; Checklists for salesmen____; Checklists for importers____; Checklists for issuing banks____; Checklists for advising banks____; Checklists for the exporter on receipt of the credit____; Difficulties on presentation of documents____; Transferable credits____; Back-to-back credits____; Revolving credits____; Red clause credits____; Definition of a bill of exchange____; Using bills of exchange____; D/P____; D/A ____; Clean collections____; *Uniform Rules for Collections*____; Collection charges____; Protest____; Open-account transactions____; Financing overseas trade by own resources____; Overdrafts____; Loans____; Negotiation of bills____; Discounting of bills_____; London acceptance credits_____; ECGD guarantees_____; Non-recourse finance_____; Factoring_____; Invoice discounting_____; Medium-term finance_____; Long-term finance_____; Finance of imports_____; ECGD policies_____; Comprehensive short-term guarantees_____; Specific policies _____; Bank guarantees_____; Lines of credit guarantees_____; Bond support schemes_____; Pledges_____; Letters of hypothecation_____; SITPRO aligned documentation_____;

9.3 Useful addresses and publications

There are many useful publications and handbooks which should be available in every office. It is false economy not to have these publications available, and not to be on the relevant mailing lists to receive updated copies as they become available. Students are strongly recommended to buy personal copies of the smaller ones, but also to insist that offices have copies available.

International Chamber of Commerce publications

The following publications of the International Chamber of Commerce are essential reading. They are obtainable from ICC (Brochures Department), Centre Point, 103 New Oxford Street, London WC1A 1QB (01-240 5558).

Guide to Incoterms 1980

Uniform Customs and Practice for Documentary Credits, publication no. 290 (see Appendix A)

Uniform Rules for Collections, publication no. 322 (see Appendix B).

Credit control and trade indemnity credit insurance

For information on credit control and trade indemnity credit insurance see *Stubbs Gazette* and the *Dun & Bradstreet Register*. Dun & Bradstreet Ltd, 26–32 Clifton Street, London EC2P 2LY (01-247 4377).

Trade Indemnity PLC, 12–34 Great Eastern Street, London EC2A 3AX (01-739 4311).

Simplification of international trade procedures

For advice on documentation, particularly aligned documentation, consult SITPRO, Almack House, King Street, London SW1Y 6QW (01-214 3399).

They also sell excellent checklists about letters of credit and two handbooks entitled *Systematic Export Documentation*

Export documents

For supplies of export forms of every sort, particularly bills of exchange, SITPRO master documents, etc., consult Formecon Services Ltd, Douglas House, Gateway, Crewe CW1 1YN.

Export and import handbooks

The standard reference work on export matters is Croner's *Reference Book for Exporters*, available from Croner Publications Ltd, Croner House, 173 Kingston Road, New Malden, Surrey KT3 3SS. There is also a handbook entitled *Reference Book for Importers*.

Other titles in the 'Elements of Overseas Trade Series'

This book is one of a series which covers the various aspects of the Foundation Course in Overseas Trade. The other titles in the series are:

Elements of Cargo Insurance, Dennis Badger and Geoffrey Whitehead;
Elements of Export Law, Geoffrey Whitehead;
Elements of Transportation and Documentation, Ralph Bugg and Geoffrey Whitehead;
Elements of Export Marketing, John Stapleton.

These will be available from booksellers. If you have any difficulty obtaining copies, please write to the publishers at the address shown in the front of this book for the name of your nearest stockist.

Other useful texts

For bankers who have a special interest in overseas trade and payments, the standard work is *Finance of International Trade*, by Alasdair Watson, published by the Institute of Bankers, and distributed by Woodhead-Faulkner Ltd, 17 Market Street, Cambridge CB2 3PA.

A useful booklet on finance for overseas trade is *Money for Business*, issued jointly by the Economist Intelligence Unit, Bank of England and the City Communications Centre, 7th Floor, The Stock Exchange, London EC2N 1HP.

Students interested in following the theory of international trade will find a clear explanation in *Economics Made Simple*, written by Geoffrey Whitehead and published by William Heinemann Ltd.

Professional qualifications: Institute addresses

All those engaged in overseas trade should seek to acquire full professional qualifications. The five chief institutes to whom enquiries about membership should be addressed are as follows:

(*a*) The Institute of Export, World Trade Centre, London E1 9AA (01-488 4766).
(*b*) The Institute of Freight Forwarders, Suffield House, 9 Paradise Road, Richmond, Surrey TW9 1SA (01-948 3141).
(*c*) The Society of Shipping Executives, 24 Ormond Road, Richmond, Surrey TW10 6TH (01-948 4151).
(*d*) The Institute of Marketing, Moor Hall, Cookham, Maidenhead, Berkshire SL6 9QH (Maidenhead (0628) 24922).
(*e*) The Chartered Insurance Institute, 31 Hillcrest Road, London E18 2JP (01-989 8464).

Appendix A
Uniform Customs and Practice for Documentary Credits

International Chamber of Commerce publication no. 290 (1974)
General provisions and definitions

(*a*) These provisions and definitions and the following Articles apply to all documentary credits and are binding upon all parties thereto unless otherwise expressly agreed.
(*b*) For the purposes of such provisions, definitions and Articles, the expressions 'documentary credit(s)' and 'credit(s)' used therein mean any arrangement, however named or described, whereby a bank (the issuing bank), acting at the request and in accordance with the instructions of a customer (the applicant for the credit):
i is to make payment to or to the order of a third party (the beneficiary), or is to pay, accept or negotiate bills of exchange (drafts) drawn by the beneficiary, *or*
ii authorises such payments to be made or such drafts to be paid, accepted or negotiated by another bank, against stipulated documents, provided that the terms and conditions of the credit are complied with.
(*c*) Credits, by their nature, are separate transactions from the sales or other contracts on which they may be based and banks are in no way concerned with or bound by such contracts.
(*d*) Credit instructions and the credits themselves must be complete and precise.
In order to guard against confusion and misunderstanding, issuing banks should discourage any attempt by the applicant for the credit to include excessive detail.
(*e*) A bank authorised to pay, accept or negotiate under a credit shall be the bank first entitled to exercise the option available under Article 32(b). The decision of such bank shall bind all parties concerned
A bank is authorised to pay or accept under a credit by being specifically nominated in the credit

A bank is authorised to negotiate under a credit either
i by being specifically nominated in the credit, *or*
ii by the credit being freely negotiable by any bank.

(*f*) A beneficiary can in no case avail himself of the contractual relationships existing between banks or between the applicant for the credit and the issuing bank.

A Form and notification of credits

Article 1

(*a*) Credits may be either
i revocable, *or*
ii irrevocable.

(*b*) All credits, therefore, should clearly indicate whether they are revocable or irrevocable.

(*c*) In the absence of such indication, the credit shall be deemed to be revocable.

Article 2

A revocable credit may be amended or cancelled at any moment without prior notice to the beneficiary. However, the issuing bank is bound to reimburse a branch or other bank to which such a credit has been transmitted and made available for payment, acceptance or negotiation, for any payment, acceptance or negotiation complying with the terms and conditions of the credit and any amendments received up to the time of payment, acceptance or negotiation made by such branch or other bank prior to receipt by it of notice of amendment or cancellation.

Article 3

(*a*) An irrevocable credit constitutes a definite undertaking of the issuing bank, provided that the terms and conditions of the credit are complied with:

i to pay, or that payment will be made if the credit provides for payment, whether against a draft or not

ii to accept drafts if the credit provides for acceptance by the issuing bank or to be responsible for their acceptance and payment at maturity if the credit provides for the acceptance of drafts drawn on the applicant for the credit or any other drawee specified in the credit

iii to purchase/negotiate, without recourse to drawers and/or bona fide holders, drafts drawn by the beneficiary, at sight or at a tenor, on the applicant for the credit or on any other drawee specified in the credit, or to provide for purchase/negotiation by another bank, if the credit provides for purchase/negotiation.

(*b*) An irrevocable credit may be advised to a beneficiary through another bank (the advising bank) without engagement on the part of that bank, but when an issuing bank authorises or requests another bank to confirm its irrevocable credit and the latter does so, such confirmation constitutes a definite undertaking of the confirming bank in addition to the undertaking of the issuing bank, provided that the terms and conditions of the credit are complied with:

i to pay, if the credit is payable at its own counters, whether against a draft or not, or that payment will be made if the credit provides for payment elsewhere

ii to accept drafts if the credit provides for acceptance by the confirming bank, at its own counters, or to be responsible for their acceptance and payment at maturity if the credit provides for the acceptance of drafts drawn on the applicant for the credit or any other drawee specified in the credit

iii to purchase/negotiate without recourse to drawers and/or bona fide holders, drafts drawn by the beneficiary, at sight or at a tenor, on the issuing bank, or on the applicant for the credit or on any other drawee specified in the credit, if the credit provides for purchase/negotiation.

(*c*) Such undertakings can be neither amended nor cancelled without the agreement of all parties thereto. Partial acceptance of amendments is not effective without the agreement of all parties thereto.

Article 4

(*a*) When an issuing bank instructs a bank by cable, telegram or telex to advise a credit, and intends the mail confirmation to be the operative credit instrument, the cable, telegram or telex must state that the credit will only be effective on receipt of such mail confirmation. In this event, the issuing bank must send the operative credit instrument (mail confirmation) and any subsequent amendments to the credit to the beneficiary through the advising bank.

(*b*) The issuing bank will be responsible for any consequences arising from its failure to follow the procedure set out in the preceding paragraph.

(*c*) Unless a cable, telegram or telex states 'details to follow' (or words of similar effect), or states that the mail confirmation is to be the operative credit instrument, the cable, telegram or telex will be deemed to be the operative credit instrument and the issuing bank need not send the mail confirmation to the advising bank.

Article 5

When a bank is instructed by cable, telegram or telex to issue, confirm or advise a credit similar in terms to one previously established and which has been the subject of amendments, it shall be understood that the details of the credit being issued, confirmed or advised will be transmitted to the beneficiary excluding the amendments, unless the instructions specify clearly any amendments which are to apply.

Article 6

If incomplete or unclear instructions are received to issue, confirm or advise a credit, the bank requested to act on such instructions may give preliminary notification of the credit to the beneficiary for information only and without responsibility; in this event the credit will be issued, confirmed or advised only when the necessary information has been received.

B Liabilities and responsibilities

Article 7

Banks must examine all documents with reasonable care to ascertain that they appear on their face to be in accordance with the terms and conditions of the credit. Documents which appear on their face to be inconsistent with one another will be considered as not appearing on their face to be in accordance with the terms and conditions of the credit.

Article 8

(*a*) In documentary credit operations all parties concerned deal in documents and not in goods.

(*b*) Payment, acceptance or negotiation against documents which appear on their face to be in accordance with the terms and conditions of a credit by a bank authorised to do so, binds the party giving the authorisation to take up the documents and reimburse the bank which has affected the payment, acceptance or negotiation.

(*c*) If, upon receipt of the documents, the issuing bank considers that they appear on their face not to be in accordance with the terms and conditions of the credit, that bank must determine, on the basis of the documents alone, whether to claim that payment, acceptance or negotiation was not effected in accordance with the terms and conditions of the credit.

(*d*) The issuing bank shall have a reasonable time to examine the documents and to determine as above whether to make such a claim.

(*e*) If such claim is to be made, notice to that effect, stating the reasons therefor, must, without delay, be given by cable or other expeditious means to the bank from which the documents have been received (the remitting bank) and such notice must state that the documents are being held at the disposal of such bank or are being returned thereto.

(*f*) If the issuing bank fails to hold the documents at the disposal of the remitting bank, or fails to return the documents to such bank, the issuing bank shall be precluded from claiming that the relative payment, acceptance or negotiation was not effected in accordance with the terms and conditions of the credit.

(*g*) If the remitting bank draws the attention of the issuing bank to any irregularities in the documents or advises such bank that it has paid, accepted or negotiated under reserve or against a guarantee in respect of such irregularities, the issuing bank shall not thereby be relieved from any of its obligations under this Article. Such guarantee or reserve concerns only the relations between the remitting bank and beneficiary.

Article 9

Banks assume no liability or responsibility for the form, sufficiency, accuracy, genuineness, falsification or legal effect of any documents, or for the general and/or particular conditions stipulated in the documents or superimposed thereon; nor do they assume any liability or responsibility for the description, quantity, weight, quality, condition, packing, delivery, value or existence of the goods represented thereby, or for the good faith or acts and/or omissions, solvency, performance or standing of the consignor, the carriers or the insurers of the goods or any other person whomsoever.

Article 10

Banks assume no liability or responsibility for the consequences arising out of delay and/or loss in transit of any messages, letters or documents, or for delay, mutilation or other errors arising in the transmission of cables, telegrams or telex. Banks assume no liability or responsibility for errors in translation or interpretation of technical terms, and reserve the right to transmit credit terms without translating them.

Article 11

Banks assume no liability or responsibility for consequences arising out of the interruption of their business by acts of God, riots, civil commotions, insurrections, wars or any other causes beyond their control or by any strikes or lockouts. Unless specifically authorised, banks will not effect payment, acceptance or negotiation after expiration under credits expiring during such interruption of business.

Article 12

(*a*) Banks utilising the services of another bank for the purpose of giving effect to the instructions of the applicant for the credit do so for the account and at the risk of the latter.

(*b*) Banks assume no liability or responsibility should the instructions they transmit not be carried out, even if they have themselves taken the initiative in the choice of such other bank.

(*c*) The applicant for the credit shall be bound by and liable to indemnify the banks against all obligations and responsibilities imposed by foreign laws and usages.

Article 13

A paying or negotiating bank which has been authorised to claim reimbursement from a third bank nominated by the issuing bank and which has effected such payment or negotiation shall not be required to confirm to the third bank that it has done so in accordance with the terms and conditions of the credit.

C Documents

Article 14

(*a*) All instructions to issue, confirm or advise a credit must state precisely the documents against which payment, acceptance or negotiation is to be made.

(*b*) Terms such as 'first class', 'well known', 'qualified' and the like shall not be used to describe the issuers of any documents called for under credits and if they are incorporated in the credit terms banks will accept documents as tendered.

C.1 Documents evidencing shipment or despatch or taking in charge (shipping documents)

Article 15

Except as stated in Article 20, the date of the bill of lading, or the date of any other document evidencing shipment or despatch or taking in charge, or the date indicated in the reception stamp or by notation on any such document, will be taken in each case to be the date of shipment or despatch or taking in charge of the goods.

Article 16

(*a*) If words clearly indicating payment or prepayment of freight, however named or described, appear by stamp or otherwise on documents evidencing shipment or despatch they will be accepted as constituting evidence of payment of freight.
(*b*) If the words 'freight pre-payable' or 'freight to be prepaid' or words of similar effect appear by stamp or otherwise on such documents they will not be accepted as constituting evidence of the payment of freight.
(*c*) Unless otherwise specified in the credit or inconsistent with any of the documents presented under the credit, banks will accept documents stating that freight or transportation charges are payable on delivery.
(*d*) Banks will accept shipping documents bearing reference by stamp or otherwise to costs additional to the freight charges, such as costs of, or disbursements incurred in connection with, loading, unloading or similar operations, unless the conditions of the credit specifically prohibit such reference.

Article 17

Shipping documents which bear a clause on the face thereof such as 'shipper's load and count' or 'said by shipper to contain' or words of similar effect, will be accepted unless otherwise specified in the credit.

Article 18

(*a*) A clean shipping document is one which bears no superimposed clause or notation which expressly declares a defective condition of the goods and/or the packaging.
(*b*) Banks will refuse shipping documents bearing such clauses or notations unless the credit expressly states the clauses or notations which may be accepted.

C.1.1 Marine bills of lading

Article 19

(*a*) Unless specifically authorised in the credit, bills of lading of the following nature will be rejected:

i bills of lading issued by forwarding agents
ii bills of lading which are issued under and are subject to the conditions of a charter-party
iii bills of lading covering shipment by sailing vessels.

(*b*) However, subject to the above and unless otherwise specified in the credit, bills of lading of the following nature will be accepted:

i 'through' bills of lading issued by shipping companies or their agents even though they cover several modes of transport

ii short form bills of lading (i.e. bills of lading issued by shipping companies or their agents which indicate some or all of the conditions of carriage by reference to a source or document other than the bill of lading)

iii bills of lading issued by shipping companies or their agents covering unitised cargoes, such as those on pallets or in containers.

Article 20

(*a*) Unless otherwise specified in the credit, bills of lading must show that the goods are loaded on board a named vessel or shipped on a named vessel.
(*b*) Loading on board a named vessel or shipment on a named vessel may be evidenced either by a bill of lading bearing wording indicating loading on board a named vessel or shipment on a named vessel, or by means of a notation to that effect on the bill of lading signed or initialled and dated by the carrier or his agent, and the date of this notation shall be regarded as the date of loading on board the named vessel or shipment on the named vessel.

Article 21

(*a*) Unless trans-shipment is prohibited by the terms of the credit, bills of lading will be accepted which indicate that the goods will be trans-shipped en route, provided the entire voyage is covered by one and the same bill of lading.
(*b*) Bills of lading incorporating printed clauses stating that the carriers have the right to trans-ship will be accepted notwithstanding the fact that the credit prohibits trans-shipment.

Article 22

(*a*) Banks will refuse a bill of lading stating that the goods are loaded on deck, unless specifically authorised in the credit.
(*b*) Banks will not refuse a bill of lading which contains a provision that the goods may be carried on deck, provided it does not specifically state that they are loaded on deck.

C1.2 Combined transport documents

Article 23

(*a*) If the credit calls for a combined transport document, i.e. one which provides for a combined transport by at least two different modes of transport, from a place at which the goods are taken in charge to a place designated for delivery, or if the credit provides for a combined transport, but in either case does not specify the form of document required and/or the issuer of such document, banks will accept such documents as tendered.
(*b*) If the combined transport includes transport by sea the document will be accepted although it does not indicate that the goods are on board a

named vessel, and although it contains a provision that the goods, if packed in a container, may be carried on deck, provided it does not specifically state that they are loaded on deck.

C.1.3 Other shipping documents, etc.

Article 24

Banks will consider a railway or inland waterway bill of lading or consignment note, counterfoil waybill, postal receipt, certificate of mailing, air mail receipt, air waybill, air consignment note or air receipt, trucking company bill of lading or any other similar document as regular when such document bears the reception stamp of the carrier or his agent, or when it bears a signature purporting to be that of the carrier or his agent.

Article 25

Where a credit calls for an attestation or certification of weight in the case of transport other than by sea, banks will accept a weight stamp or declaration of weight superimposed by the carrier on the shipping document unless the credit calls for a separate or independent certificate of weight.

C.2 Insurance documents

Article 26

(*a*) Insurance documents must be as specified in the credit and must be issued and/or signed by insurance companies or their agents or by underwriters.
(*b*) Cover notes issued by brokers will not be accepted, unless specifically authorised in the credit.

Article 27

Unless otherwise specified in the credit, or unless the insurance documents presented establish that the cover is effective at the latest from the date of shipment or despatch or, in the case of combined transport, the date of taking the goods in charge, banks will refuse insurance documents presented which bear a date later than the date of shipment or despatch or, in the case of combined transport, the date of taking the goods in charge, as evidenced by the shipping documents.

Article 28

(*a*) Unless otherwise specified in the credit, the insurance document must be expressed in the same currency as the credit.
(*b*) The minimum amount for which insurance must be effected is the CIF value of the goods concerned. However, when the CIF value of the goods cannot be determined from the documents on their face, banks will accept as such minimum amount the amount of the drawing under the credit or the amount of the relative commercial invoice, whichever is the greater.

Article 29

(*a*) Credits should expressly state the type of insurance required and, if any,

the additional risks which are to be covered. Imprecise terms such as 'usual risks' or 'customary risks' should not be used; however, if such imprecise terms are used, banks will accept insurance documents as tendered.
(*b*) Failing specific instructions, banks will accept insurance cover as tendered.

Article 30

Where a credit stipulates 'insurance against all risks', banks will accept an insurance document which contains any 'all risks' notation or clause, and will assume no responsibility if any particular risk is not covered.

Article 31

Banks will accept an insurance document which indicates that the cover is subject to a franchise or an excess (deductible) unless it is specifically stated in the credit that the insurance must be issued irrespective of percentage.

C.3 Commercial invoices

Article 32

(*a*) Unless otherwise specified in the credit, commercial invoices must be made out in the name of the applicant for the credit.
(*b*) Unless otherwise specified in the credit, banks may refuse commercial invoices issued for amounts in excess of the amount permitted by the credit.
(*c*) The description of the goods in the commercial invoice must correspond with the description in the credit. In all other documents the goods may be described in general terms not inconsistent with the description of the goods in the credit.

C.4 Other documents

Article 33

When other documents are required, such as warehouse receipts, delivery orders, consular invoices, certificates of origin, of weight, of quality or of analysis, etc., and when no further definition is given, banks will accept such documents as tendered.

D Miscellaneous provisions
Quantity and amount

Article 34

(*a*) The words 'about', 'circa' or similar expressions used in connection with the amount of the credit or the quantity or the unit price of the goods are to be construed as allowing a difference not to exceed 10 per cent more or 10 per cent less.
(*b*) Unless a credit stipulates that the quantity of the goods specified must not be exceeded or reduced a tolerance of 3 per cent more or 3 per cent less will be permissible, always provided that the total amount of the drawings does not exceed the amount of the credit. This tolerance does not apply

when the credit specifies quantity in terms of a stated number of packing units or individual items.

Partial shipments

Article 35

(*a*) Partial shipments are allowed, unless the credit specifically states otherwise.
(*b*) Shipments made on the same ship and for the same voyage, even if the bills of lading evidencing shipment 'on board' bear different dates and/or indicate different ports of shipment, will not be regarded as partial shipments.

Article 36

If shipment by instalments within given periods is stipulated and any instalment is not shipped within the period allowed for that instalment, the credit ceases to be available for that or any subsequent instalments, unless otherwise specified in the credit.

Expiry date

Article 37

All credits, whether revocable or irrevocable, must stipulate an expiry date for presentation of documents for payment, acceptance or negotiation, notwithstanding the stipulation of a latest date for shipment.

Article 38

The words 'to', 'until', 'till', and words of similar import applying to the stipulated expiry date for presentation of documents for payment, acceptance or negotiation, or to the stipulated latest date for shipment, will be understood to include the date mentioned.

Article 39

(*a*) When the stipulated expiry date falls on a day on which banks are closed for reasons other than those mentioned in Article 11, the expiry date will be extended until the first following business day.
(*b*) The latest date for shipment shall not be extended by reason of the extension of the expiry date in accordance with this Article. Where the credit stipulates a latest date for shipment, shipping documents dated later than such stipulated date will not be accepted. If no latest date for shipment is stipulated in the credit, shipping documents dated later than the expiry date stipulated in the credit or amendments thereto will not be accepted. Documents other than the shipping documents may, however, be dated up to and including the extended expiry date.
(*c*) Banks paying, accepting or negotiating on such extended expiry date must add to the documents their certification in the following wording:

> 'presented for payment (or acceptance or negotiation as the case may be) within the expiry date extended in accordance with Article 39 of the *Uniform Customs*'.

Shipment, loading or despatch

Article 40

(*a*) Unless the terms of the credit indicate otherwise, the words, 'departure', 'despatch', 'loading' or 'sailing' used in stipulating the latest date for shipment of the goods will be understood to be synonymous with 'shipment'.
(*b*) Expressions such as 'prompt', 'immediately', 'as soon as possible' and the like should not be used. If they are used, banks will interpret them as a request for shipment within thirty days from the date on the advice of the credit to the beneficiary by the issuing bank or by an advising bank, as the case may be.
(*c*) The expression 'on or about' and similar expressions will be interpreted as a request for shipment during the period from five days before to five days after the specified date, both end days included.

Presentation

Article 41

Notwithstanding the requirement of Article 37 that every credit must stipulate an expiry date for presentation of documents, credits must also stipulate a specified period of time after the date of issuance of the bills of lading or other shipping documents during which presentation of documents for payment, acceptance or negotiation must be made. If no such period of time is stipulated in the credit, banks will refuse documents presented to them later than 21 days after the date of issuance of the bills of lading or other shipping documents.

Article 42

Banks are under no obligation to accept presentation of documents outside their banking hours.

Date terms

Article 43

The terms 'first half', 'second half' of a month shall be construed respectively as from the 1st to the 15th, and the 16th to the last day of each month, inclusive.

Article 44

The terms 'beginning', 'middle' or 'end' of a month shall be construed respectively as from the 1st to the 10th, the 11th to the 20th, and the 21st to the last day of each month, inclusive.

Article 45

When a bank issuing a credit instructs that the credit be confirmed or advised as available 'for one month', 'for six months', or the like, but does not specify the date from which the time is to run, the confirming or advising bank will confirm or advise the credit as expiring at the end of such indicated period from the date of its confirmation or advice.

E Transfer

Article 46

(*a*) A transferable credit is a credit under which the beneficiary has the right to give instructions to the bank called upon to effect payment or acceptance or to any bank entitled to effect negotiation to make the credit available in whole or in part to one or more third parties (second beneficiaries).
(*b*) The bank requested to effect the transfer, whether it has confirmed the credit or not, shall be under no obligation to effect such transfer except to the extent and in the manner expressly consented to by such bank, and until such bank's charges in respect of transfer are paid.
(*c*) Bank charges in respect of transfers are payable by the first beneficiary unless otherwise specified.
(*d*) A credit can be transferred only if it is expressly designated as 'transferable' by the issuing bank. Terms such as 'divisible', 'fractionable', 'assignable', and 'transmissible' add nothing to the meaning of the term 'transferable' and shall not be used.
(*e*) A transferable credit can be transferred once only. Fractions of a transferable credit (not exceeding in the aggregate the amount of the credit) can be transferred separately, provided partial shipments are not prohibited, and the aggregate of such transfers will be considered as constituting only one transfer of the credit. The credit can be transferred only on the terms and conditions specified in the original credit, with the exception of the amount of the credit, of any unit prices stated therein, and of the period of validity or period for shipment, any or all of which may be reduced or curtailed. Additionally, the name of the first beneficiary can be substituted for that of the applicant for the credit, but if the name of the applicant for the credit is specifically required by the original credit to appear in any document other than the invoice, such requirement must be fulfilled.
(*f*) The first beneficiary has the right to substitute his own invoices for those of the second beneficiary, for amounts not in excess of the original amount stipulated in the credit and for the original unit prices if stipulated in the credit, and upon such substitution of invoices the first beneficiary can draw under the credit for the difference, if any, between his invoices and the second beneficiary's invoices. When a credit has been transferred and the first beneficiary is to supply his own invoices in exchange for the second beneficiary's invoices but fails to do so on first demand, the paying, accepting or negotiating bank has the right to deliver to the issuing bank the documents received under the credit, including the second beneficiary's invoices, without further responsibility to the first beneficiary.
(*g*) The first beneficiary of a transferable credit can transfer the credit to a second beneficiary in the same country or in another country unless the credit specifically states otherwise. The first beneficiary shall have the right to request that payment or negotiation be effected to the second beneficiary at the place to which the credit has been transferred, up to and including the

expiry date of the original credit, and without prejudice to the first beneficiary's right subsequently to substitute his own invoices for those of the second beneficiary and to claim any difference due to him.

Article 47

The fact that a credit is not stated to be transferable shall not affect the beneficiary's rights to assign the proceeds of such credit in accordance with the provisions of the applicable law.

(Reproduced by courtesy of the International Chamber of Commerce.)

Appendix B
Uniform Rules for Collections

International Chamber of Commerce publication no. 322 (1978)
General provisions and definitions

(*A*) These provisions and definitions and the following Articles apply to all collections as defined in (*B*) below and are binding upon all parties thereto unless otherwise expressly agreed or unless contrary to the provisions of a national, state or local law and/or regulation which cannot be departed from.

(*B*) For the purpose of such provisions, definitions and articles:

1 *i* 'Collection' means the handling by banks, on instructions received, of documents as defined in *ii* below, in order to:
(*a*) obtain acceptance and/or, as the case may be, payment, or
(*b*) deliver commercial documents against acceptance and/or, as the case may be, against payment, or
(*c*) deliver documents on other terms and conditions.

ii 'Documents' means financial documents and/or commercial documents:
(*a*) 'financial documents' means bills of exchange, promissory notes, cheques, payment receipts or other similar instruments used for obtaining the payment of money
(*b*) 'commercial documents' means invoices, shipping documents, documents of title or other similar documents, or any other documents whatsoever, not being financial documents.

iii 'Clean collection' means collection of financial documents not accompanied by commercial documents.

iv 'Documentary collection' means collection of:
(*a*) financial documents accompanied by commercial documents
(*b*) commercial documents not accompanied by financial documents.

2 The 'parties thereto' are:

i the 'principal', who is the customer entrusting the operation of collection to his bank *ii* the 'remitting bank', which is the bank to which the principal has entrusted the operation of collection

iii the 'collecting bank', which is any bank, other than the remitting bank, involved in processing the collection order

iv the 'presenting bank', which is the collecting bank making presentation to the drawee.

3 The 'drawee' is the one to whom presentation is to be made according to the collection order.

(*C*) All documents sent for collection must be accompanied by a collection order giving complete and precise instructions. Banks are permitted to act only upon the instructions given in such collection order, and in accordance with these rules.

If any bank cannot, for any reason, comply with the instructions given in the collection order received by it, it must immediately advise the party from whom it received the collection order.

Liabilities and responsibilities

Article 1

Banks will act in good faith and exercise reasonable care.

Article 2

Banks must verify that the documents received appear to be as listed in the collection order and must immediately advise the party from whom the collection order was received of any documents missing.

Banks have no further obligation to examine the documents.

Article 3

For the purpose of giving effect to the instructions of the principal, the remitting bank will utilise as the collecting bank:

i the collecting bank nominated by the principal, or, in the absence of such nomination,

ii any bank, of its own or another bank's choice, in the country of payment or acceptance, as the case may be.

The documents and the collection order may be sent to the collecting bank directly or through another bank as intermediary.

Banks utilising the services of other banks for the purpose of giving effect to the instructions of the principal do so for the account of and at the risk of the latter.

The principal shall be bound by and liable to indemnify the banks against all obligations and responsibilities imposed by foreign laws or usages.

Article 4

Banks concerned with a collection assume no liability or responsibility for the consequences arising out of delay and/or loss in transit of any messages, letters or documents, or for delay, mutilation or other errors arising in the transmission of cables, telegrams, telex, or communication by electronic systems, or for errors in translation or interpretation of technical terms.

Article 5

Banks concerned with a collection assume no liability or responsibility for consequences arising out of the interruption of their business by acts of God, riots, civil commotions, insurrections, wars, or any other causes beyond their control or by any strikes or lockouts.

Article 6

Goods should not be dispatched direct to the address of a bank or consigned to a bank without prior agreement on the part of that bank.

In the event of goods being dispatched direct to the address of a bank or consigned to a bank for delivery to a drawee against payment or acceptance or upon other terms without prior agreement on the part of that bank, the bank has no obligation to take delivery of the goods, which remain at the risk and responsibility of the party dispatching the goods.

Presentation

Article 7

Documents are to be presented to the drawee in the form in which they are received, except that remitting and collecting banks are authorised to affix any necessary stamps, at the expense of the principal unless otherwise instructed, and to make any necessary endorsements or place any rubber stamps or other identifying marks or symbols customary to or required for the collection operation.

Article 8

Collection orders should bear the complete address of the drawee or of the domicile at which presentation is to be made. If the address is incomplete or incorrect, the collecting bank may, without obligation and responsibility on its part, endeavour to ascertain the proper address.

Article 9

In the case of documents payable at sight the presenting bank must make presentation for payment without delay.

In the case of documents payable at a tenor other than sight the presenting bank must, where acceptance is called for, make presentation for acceptance without delay, and where payment is called for, make presentation for payment not later than the appropriate maturity date.

Article 10

In respect of a documentary collection, including a bill of exchange payable at a future date, the collection order should state whether the commercial documents are to be released to the drawee against acceptance (D/A) or against payment (D/P).

In the absence of such statement, the commercial documents will be released only against payment.

Payment

Article 11

In the case of documents payable in the currency of the country of payment (local currency), the presenting bank must, unless otherwise instructed in the collection order, only release the documents to the drawee against payment in local currency which is immediately available for disposal in the manner specified in the collection order.

Article 12

In the case of documents payable in a currency other than that of the country of payment (foreign currency) the presenting bank must, unless otherwise instructed in the collection order, only release the documents to the drawee against payment in the relative foreign currency which can immediately be remitted in accordance with the instructions given in the collection order.

Article 13

In respect of clean collections partial payments may be accepted if and to the extent to which and on the conditions on which partial payments are authorised by the law in force in the place of payment. The documents will only be released to the drawee when full payment thereof has been received.

In respect of documentary collections partial payments will be accepted only if specifically authorised in the collection order. However, unless otherwise instructed, the presenting bank will release the documents to the drawee only after full payment has been received.

In all cases partial payments will be accepted only subject to compliance with the provisions of either Article 11 or Article 12 as appropriate.

Partial payment, if accepted, will be dealt with in accordance with the provisions of Article 14.

Article 14

Amounts collected (less charges and/or disbursements and/or expenses where applicable) must be made available without delay to the bank from which the collection order was received in accordance with the instructions contained in the collection order.

Acceptance

Article 15

The presenting bank is responsible for seeing that the form of the acceptance of a bill of exchange appears to be complete and correct, but is not responsible for the genuineness of any signature or for the authority of any signatory to sign the acceptance.

Promissory notes, receipts and other similar instruments

Article 16

The presenting bank is not responsible for the genuineness of any signature or for the authority of any signatory to sign a promissory note, receipt, or other similar instrument.

Protest

Article 17

The collection order should give specific instructions regarding protest (or other legal process in lieu thereof), in the event of non-acceptance or non-payment.

In the absence of such specific instructions the banks concerned with the collection have no obligation to have the documents protested (or subjected to other legal process in lieu thereof) for non-payment or non-acceptance.

Any charges and/or expenses incurred by banks in connection with such protest or other legal process will be for the account of the principal.

Case of need (principal's representative) and protection of goods

Article 18

If the principal nominates a representative to act as case of need in the event of non-acceptance and/or non-payment the collection order should clearly and fully indicate the powers of such case of need.

In the absence of such indication banks will not accept any instructions from the case of need.

Article 19

Banks have no obligation to take any action in respect of the goods to which a documentary collection relates.

Nevertheless in the case that banks take action for the protection of the goods, whether instructed or not, they assume no liability or responsibility with regard to the fate and/or condition of the goods and/or for any acts and/or omissions on the part of any third parties entrusted with the custody and/or protection of the goods. However, the collecting bank must immediately advise the bank from which the collection order was received of any such action taken.

Any charges and/or expenses incurred by banks in connection with any action for the protection of the goods will be for the account of the principal.

Advice of fate, etc.

Article 20

Collecting banks are to advise fate in accordance with the following rules:

i Form of advice – all advices or information from the collecting bank to the bank from which the collection order was received, must bear appropriate detail including, in all cases, the latter bank's reference number of the collection order.

ii Method of advice – in the absence of specific instructions the collecting bank must send all advices to the bank from which the collection order was received by quickest mail but, if the collecting bank considers the matter to be urgent, quicker methods such as cable, telegram, telex, or communication by electronic systems, etc., may be used at the expense of the principal.

iii (*a*) Advice of payment – the collecting bank must send without delay advice of payment to the bank from which the collection order was received, detailing the amount or amounts collected, charges and/or disbursements and/or expenses deducted, where appropriate, and method of disposal of the funds.

(*b*) Advice of acceptance – the collecting bank must send without delay advice of acceptance to the bank from which the collection order was received.

(*c*) Advice of non-payment or non-acceptance – the collecting bank must send without delay advice of non-payment or advice of non-acceptance to the bank from which the collection order was received.

The presenting bank should endeavour to ascertain the reasons for such non-payment or non-acceptance and advise accordingly the bank from which the collection order was received.

On receipt of such advice the remitting bank must, within a reasonable time, give appropriate instructions as to the further handling of the documents. If such instructions are not received by the presenting bank within 90 days from its advice of non-payment or non-acceptance, the documents may be returned to the bank from which the collection order was received.

Interest, charges and expenses

Article 21

If the collection order includes an instruction to collect interest which is not embodied in the accompanying financial document(s), if any, and the drawee refuses to pay such interest, the presenting bank may deliver the document(s) against payment or acceptance as the case may be without collecting such interest, unless the collection order expressly states that such interest may not be waived. Where such interest is to be collected the collection order must bear an indication of the rate of interest and the period covered. When payment of interest has been refused the presenting bank must inform the bank from which the collection order was received accordingly.

If the documents include a financial document containing an unconditional and definitive interest clause the interest amount is deemed to form part of the amount of the documents to be collected. Accordingly, the interest amount is payable in addition to the principal amount shown in the financial document and may not be waived unless the collection order so authorises.

Article 22

If the collection order includes an instruction that collection charges and/or expenses are to be for account of the drawee and the drawee refuses to pay them, the presenting bank may deliver the document(s) against payment or acceptance as the case may be without collecting charges and/or expenses unless the collection order expressly states that such charges and/or expenses may not be waived. When payment of collection charges and/or expenses has been refused the presenting bank must inform the bank from which the collection order was received accordingly. Whenever collection charges and/or expenses are so waived they will be for the account of the principal, and may be deducted from the proceeds.

Should a collection order specifically prohibit the waiving of collection charges and/or expenses then neither the remitting nor collecting nor presenting bank shall be responsible for any costs or delays resulting from this prohibition.

Article 23

In all cases where in the express terms of a collection order, or under these rules, disbursements and/or expenses and/or collection charges are to be borne by the principal, the collecting bank(s) shall be entitled promptly to recover outlays in respect of disbursements and expenses and charges from the bank from which the collection order was received and the remitting bank shall have the right promptly to recover from the principal any amount so paid out by it, together with its own disbursements, expenses and charges, regardless of the fate of the collection.

Index